BELOVED I AM

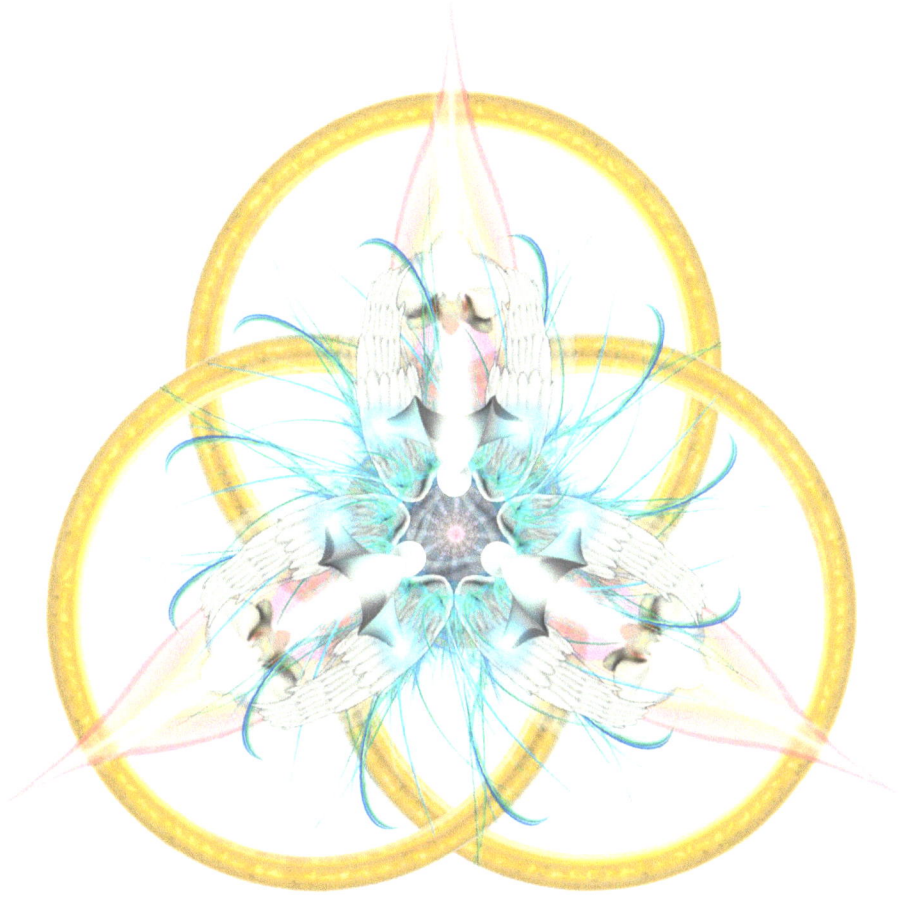

Messages from the Divine Feminine

A Collective Co-Creation of the GoldRing
www.thechristwithin.com www.premieres.com

Please Honor the Sacredness of this work

Published by: GoldRing Media LLC,
60 N 660 West,
St. George, Utah
84770

www.premieres.com

© Richard B. Wigley 2011 (Author)
© Lily Moses 2011 (Illustrator)
© Annette Laporte 2011 (Illustrator)

First edition June 2011

ISBN: 978-0-9858019-0-8

All rights reserved. With the exception of small passages quoted for review purposes, no portion of this work may be reproduced, translated, adapted, stored in a retrieval system, or transmitted in any form or through any means including electronic, mechanical, photocopying or otherwise without the written permission of the publisher.

www.thechristwithin.com

With Sacred Labor these messages are given through the love and contributions of artists, writers, editors, managers and those that hold this work in the highest intention and presence.

Written by:	**Richard B. Wigley,** Utah, United States of America
Artwork:	**Lily Moses,** Northern Rivers, New South Wales, Australia
Mandalas:	**Annette Laporte,** Ontario Canada
Project Manager:	**Annette Laporte,** Ontario Canada
Design & Typesetting:	**Annette Laporte,** Ontario, Canada **Deborah Robinson**, Alberta, Canada **Richard Wigley,** Utah USA
Editing:	**Annette Laporte**, Ontario, Canada **Jolanda de Jong**, Heerenveen, Netherlands **Nancy Wait**, Brooklyn, New York, USA **Lynne Cameron,** Port Hope, Ontario, Canada **Michel Franc,** Franklin, North Carolina
Website:	**Deborah Robinson,** Calgary Alberta Canada

BELOVED I AM
MESSAGES FROM THE DIVINE FEMININE

A Collective Co-Creation of the Gold Ring of Enlightenment and Abundance

Through destiny, fate, luck or design these visions brought together an international cooperative of inspired people. Many synchronicities and magical events surfaced during this wonderful collaboration, as the Divine Feminine Spirit behind this work expressed a will of her own and great determination to be brought forward to humanity.

Compiled in the early nineties from inner communications, the Beloved I Am, Christ Within was revealed through the simple understanding of equality. This was a time when the world was not quite ready for these activations. And so, it sat for two decades, until a few pages were read over the internet radio. Upon hearing these words, numerous listeners felt an activation of spiritual purpose. These people came together and set out to ensure these writings were published. Four of those working on the book witnessed a vision of a Heavenly Lady dressed in an opalescent gown, carrying an ankh surrounded by roses with honey bees in attendance.

On another timeline and pathway across the globe in Australia Lily Moses began to paint images of Spiritual Masters, Saints and Angels who appeared in her presence. Of these paintings came a message that it was being prepared for a book and the name, The Beloved I Am was given.

May each reader find the power within this material as transforming and as healing as we did.

FOREWARD

You are now becoming a part of a collective co-creation that reveals itself on many levels. The main message is that Christ Energy is equally and powerfully feminine in essence. This book offers an experience of immersion that embodies a number of techniques to make the transformational journey effortless. As you read and are guided through various concepts to recognize your true Divine Essence, the poetic nature of the writing as well as different font styles and word accentuations act as so many keys to opening the heart portal.

As the journey of pages unfolds, the voice moves from 1st to 2nd person, objective to subjective, personal to transcendent; speaking to heal hearts and nourish minds as this transitioning allows the reader to see the issues and concepts from personal and higher perspectives. Issues are not avoided, but are brought straight forward so they can be healed. Emotional maturity, spiritual evolution and raising of consciousness only occur when we have the strength and courage to accept, acknowledge, forgive and address the issues that bind us. Removing the beliefs that we use to hide our true selves opens new pathways into our nested layers of selfhood, expanding through the heart of compassion on our journey to self-mastery.

The detailed graphic work on each page creates a sacred space of its own to engage the aspects of the Divine Feminine. Allow yourself to be moved to and fro by the beauty within this collective co-creation, from your logical left brain into your creative right brain and engage your emotional field. Allow yourself to daydream, wander off and explore where your own mind and heart take you as you journey down these passages.

The world has known Christ as a man who walked upon the earth imparting spiritual messages of peace and love for all. The words of all spiritual traditions have been corrupted and buried through misguided patriarchy. Beloved I Am is a work of art, beauty, compassion and understanding that are offered as messages of the sacred divine feminine heart. The doorway is now open and the Divine Feminine Christ has come to offer shelter to those lost within the worlds. These sacred bestowals of unconditional love are portals to spiritual acceptance and mirrors of inspiration in which the essence of your true soul can be divinely reflected.

All humanity shares in the spirit of the Beloved I Am as the deep inner touch of knowing the Feminine Christ Within. The gentle touch of her words opens the sacred creative heart space. Through inspiration, every page heals the emotional body of fears, regrets, shame and deep loss – for both men and women. The feminine sacred heart is restored to absolute power within Christ Consciousness. Masculine spirituality listens and finds understanding of unconditional love and release as the feminine divine awakens in its heart as well. The restoration of humanity's soul unfolds through the sharing of the Love of Christ Within.

I AM the Beloved I AM, Christ Within
I AM the heart of love which calls
to you in the deepest ways.
I call to your heart, for it to open.

Allow your heart to open revealing the shining light
of the wisdom you see in the deep universe
that dwells within as you travel the infinite course to home.

I know the pain you feel in your deep heart.
I know you are alone and have given everything to be love.
I know you wish to speak. I hold my arms out to you. I am here so you
may realize where you are. I am within you.
It is true that it is the Beloved I AM that we are.

Our mystical union of divine blessings reveal truthful words of love. In power, we speak in honor and wisdom. There are no difficulties on the path. It is cleared by the intention of your Soul.

Our journey home begins.

Table of Contents

The titles of each page are presented as a Lighted Pathway where you may follow in order or intuitively select a page that is meaningful.
These words are stepping stones along the spiritual path with which you form a vibrational field and enter this sacred journey.

Section	Page	Section	Page
01. The Way	08	35. Faith	76
02. Freedom	10	36. Connection	78
03. Wisdom	12	37. Channel	80
04. Love	14	38. Remember	82
05. Sing	16	39. Learn	84
06. Purity	18	40. Center	86
07. Changes	20	41. Lesson	88
08. World	22	42. Compassion	90
09. Child	24	43. Heart	92
10. Bridge	26	44. Goddess	94
11. Forever	28	45. Approach	96
12. Energy	30	46. Within	98
13. Truth	32	47. Beloved	100
14. Transformation	34	48. Share	102
15. Conception	36	49. Healing	104
16. Essence	38	50. Give	106
17. Life	40	51. Arise	108
18. Spiritual	42	52. Unity	110
19. Realize	44	53. Seek	112
20. Awaken	46	54. Harmony	114
21. Light	48	55. Create	116
22. Voice	50	56. Breathe	118
23. Hear	52	57. Rise	120
24. The Gift	54	58. Holy	122
25. Revelation	56	59. Mystery	124
26. Home	58	60. Immaculate	126
27. Reflection	60	61. Closeness	128
28. Asking	62	62. Feel	130
29. Open	64	63. Opening	132
30. Accept	66	64. Begin	134
31. Feeling	68	65. Human	136
32. Experience	70	66. Emotion	138
33. Transition	72	67. Perfect	140
34. Communion	74	68. I Am	142
		69. Treasure	144

The Heavenly Rose

BELOVED ~  ~ I AM

The Way

pen up your mind to your inner teacher and let this teacher bring you to a greater understanding. This inner teacher is your Christ Within.

The Christ Within speaks to you as god and goddess, male and female, and from the center where there is only love, your heart.

Allow your mind to walk past your boundaries. Feel the distinctions between bodies and ideas fade away. Feel with your heart this Information, Light and Wisdom

Go beyond what you have read and have been taught. Listen to the words. Watch as they enter and see them. Be patient and wait for the answers to your questions. Build up trust and have the integrity to hold the character you have begun to express. Allow yourself perfection in this moment.

Your nature is as clean and pure
as White Starlight and is
reflective of Divine Wisdom
I wish perfection for you
In my eyes you are perfect
I see only your light

The wisdom and understanding you wish for is yours. Open up and see Christ in each person, in the very center, within. If it is your intent to bring love into your heart, see it, feel it, and know it in all others.

Open your eyes to light. It is all around you, even as your Eyes are closed. Know that I am with you. You are given this knowledge in every instance.

In your mind you face constant boundaries and say they are "reality." You are just imagining them and then thinking these limitations are real. The reality is you are Free Beyond Boundaries. Imagine this instead.

Open the channel to your heart center
Allow your body to feel emotion

This is what you can do
You are free to accept love
Ask for love before all

Beloved I AM
the
Christ Within

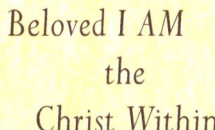

The Christ Within can only bring you forgiveness and release. You are not evil, poor or hurtful.

You are always loved and cared for. You are not in shame, you are always forgiven and always seen in the light. The truth is you have forgotten your higher powers.

There has been a mistake made here. The mistake is based in emotions. The emotions have been subverted. Emotions are not bad, but there is a difference between positive and negative emotions.

Negative emotions have become food of those beings that wish to take power from you, rather than receiving it from the Source of All Creation. This possession is evil because it is based in fear, not in love. It is based in separation from Source. It is allowed, but it is selfishness and not appropriate for you.

I bring you happiness, not pain. Pain is the false doctrine. You are forgiven of your fear of God. The Infinite Creator only loves you and wants your return. The Infinite Creator's love will never hurt you.

COME HOME

BELOVED ~   ~ I AM

freedom

 **E**very second of your Time is of value. Achieve all your wishes and know you are here for a purpose. You are here to receive and enable the presence of the Christ Within.

You are here to give love to the world, and reestablish nourishment. Support the earth and yourself.

Accept a Higher Sphere Of Life
Accept your freedom

You have been within the struggle of the lesson of karma. Peace has seemed forbidden to you. It is your time to rise up and achieve the higher vision by not being interested in yourself.

You have always seemed interested in yourself. Even in pain you are interested in how you will do this, and how you will do that? Forget self and think only of light and love. Forgetting of self will enable you to bring in the stream of love, and hold it with greater fullness and power.

There are those that doubt the coming of the stream of love at this time. They scoff at it like it were another event, but it is not. This time or the millennium does not matter; consciousness is the key. The energy has always been ready to unfold.

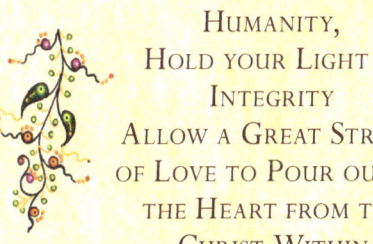

HUMANITY,
HOLD YOUR LIGHT IN
INTEGRITY
ALLOW A GREAT STREAM
OF LOVE TO POUR OUT OF
THE HEART FROM THE
CHRIST WITHIN

 Think of the larger plan. Your first thought must be trust. This is not possible, as long as a majority of humanity remain closed, oblivious and ignorant to the nature and sacredness of life. Thinking this is less than human, because it is selfish.

Trust is the first Truth

Material life must be given its place. It is the place of action. Understand and trust your will and desires. Creation is good. Create a lighter physical world.

Your world is completing a cycle. It is coming easily. The world can be completed in many different ways. The end of the mystery is upon you, but there are many probabilities.

You are here to Bring about The Greater Light

The world is changing because it has reached a state of critical mass. All energy is being focused into the earth so that it may change and follow a new direction. The probability for your world to go in the direction of greater light is available, as well as for it to move into greater darkness. You are either building or destroying your world.

All things are Possible

You are working for more Space,

more Life and more Freedom

Accept Life

Atlanto

Beloved ~   ~ I AM

Wisdom

Wisdom raises your vibrations when you hear it, see it, feel it and know its wealth. The Wealth you truly are is spectacular. You have the wealth of a thousand worlds.

Bring to Earth a new Picture of Reality

Trust and believe you are given the ability to serve. Follow your inner guidance. Hold onto your emotion and be directed by the Christ Within to the heart of your consciousness.

You have come here for a reason. Allow yourself the freedom in this space to take hold and break free from your barriers.

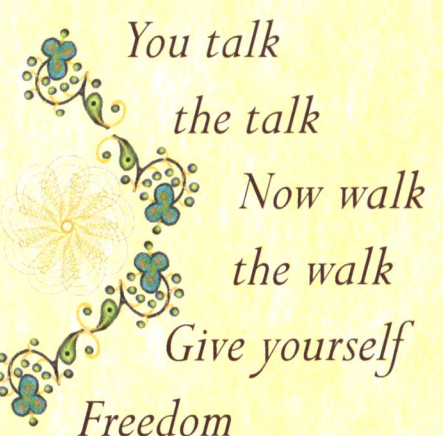

You talk the talk
Now walk the walk
Give yourself Freedom

You are close, but still you mistrust the one who would lead you. Listen and take this advice, for your Guidance Is Within you. Allow Christ to be here within you.

See with a greater vision. Allow the voice to come through you and bring your mind to hear. Respond to the thoughts you listen to.

They may come in emotional, financial, scientific, or everyday terms, in every realm you know, you will understand. Sounds, colors, words, symbols, feelings, all the intricate details of your world are the language.

Bring symbols and shapes to create a clear picture of what is needed so you may advance.

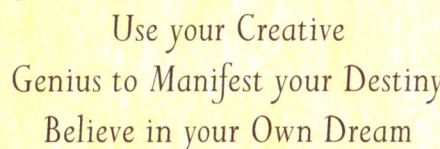

Use your Creative Genius to Manifest your Destiny
Believe in your Own Dream

The outer world does not change. It is without life, without freedom, and is tormented with constant struggle and pain. Are you ready to live in faith and trust, opening up to your inner feelings? Do you doubt this feeling? Are these questions you ask yourself? Know there can be no avoidance of experience, only denial.

Will you Show yourself to me so I know this is not My Imagination?
Is this your question?
Allow your own Journey within. I am behind and Within all Things

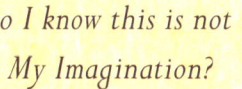

Say, "I Am Ready to See **fEEL & KNOW** This is the Truth."

Each lesson must be learned, then there is awakening. Allow the reality to change within you first, and then see the outer change.

Ask the right questions. The answers are not only here, but they are knocking at your door. Open it! There is no barrier to hold back the Christ Within.

Allow for freedom and for time to break away from the past. Release the weight of fear and rise up. Speak the truth that comes from the Christ Within.

Seraphim

BELOVED ~   LOVE   ~ I AM

In your soul, let go of all that keeps it weighted down. Let go of the hold to the physical plane. Rise faster and higher.

Trust and Know in whatever you do, I Am here to be with you and guide you

There is something you must consciously deal with, the sense of worthlessness.

I am with you to guide you into the light of your own self. You are a Powerful Spiritual Being, nothing less.

You are one with the light, and as great as I am, this is the dream that you have. Open your eyes and see it, and you will know this. It is nothing like you think it is. You have not seen this light before.

Your world is tied to dramas of the past. Know they are over.

Feel Light Nurture your Mind and Give you purpose. You are beginning to Trust. You are being Drawn into Higher Dimensions of Life Experiences

I am here to walk with you into the light. I am here, so you will trust and see this time. I am here for you. Be in your power. You are empowered and willing to step up.

Be the one who will speak truth with clarity. Others are doing this as well. There are others who sing the song, but your part is just as valuable and beautiful.

There is something you are showing the world. I want to know and be part of your world. I speak your name and know you have heard me. You are doing what I wish for you to do. Follow the Highest.

Follow your Heart to LOVE

I am in your service, I am here to bring your mind to oneness. You are here to bring light into your heart. You do this by feeling the light of your love pouring into your heart, where it burns with an eternal flame.

I can hear you always speak of love, growth and peace. You hold no fear or hopelessness. In your heart is faith and love living like this is your dream, to live without secrets, without darkness and to provide safety for others.

All you need to know is you are judged worthy. I am worthy to be a master and servant. I am honored by your work and your love. I am known in your world as the Christ.

I am the teacher of consciousness. In this way I am here to bring you love. You have never known this love before, for it would have shattered your experience and ended your lesson.

What I speak of you know nothing of yet you are the pure joy of heaven This is something to be proud of.

Open up to feeling Remember the Voices and the Dream of the Experience Of Love

Beloved ~   ~ I AM

Sing

Remember the song of one voice, hearing one mind knowing goodness and willing one thought.

This is the dream for all who suffer in diversity. You know I walk you into the light. The love you wish to express is there, but the feeling you want to share is not there yet. This awaits your acceptance, before you may go onward.

Take the next step, hold the tune and Sing. Show others your peace and happiness. Love moves on beams of light, always moving even if your eyes are unopened. Let your eyes see and let your heart feel. You have both eyes and a Heart. You cannot close them from the Song.

Journey inside to appreciate yourself. I Am Christ, I appreciate you in every way. I Am Christ, I Am the Christ Within guarding your way into the very depth of your being.

Know you are

Loved & Appreciated

by Yourself as Christ Within

Do not allow the world to see you without peace. Without peace you are nothing but a jumble of nerves and fears walking away from light in fear.

Be stronger and more sure. Hold tightly on the strings of the world and bind yourself to higher thoughts.

I will guide you and hold you in completion of the spiritual. Hold onto the physical and emotional world so you can play the song of creation within the mental world.

This is the Greatest Gift I Give You
See the Truth in the World
It is the Will of Source
The Way of the Light

Nature is in every

Place at every Time

Truth Gives Peace

I Am in Peace and Happiness

I Accept Grace and I Accept

My Value and Worthiness

The Source of All Creation knows better than I, for Source created life. In life I am given conscious awareness of Spirit and Soul. Consciousness is diminished when hidden in darkness.

Love your Creator. This is all you can do. You cannot be the equal of the Infinite Creator. You feel humbled and afraid because you have no gifts fit for the Source of All Creation except your love. You are in the throes of pain. Life is your gift, be comforted by the eternal Love you are given.

You feel and say in every way you are not good enough. You are good at being this or that, proud of your things, powerful in the world, but in your heart of hearts you are afraid you are unworthy and you fear rejection.

This is the truth that you are hearing, and in this pain you strive to be better. The fact remains we are not our own creator. We are creation and are co-creators. This is who you are. Love this part of who you are. You are part of me.

Created Beings Will
Always Be Creation
Be Comforted,
You will always
Be Loved

Archangel Michael

Beloved ~　　~ I AM

Purity

nter upon the sacred journey.
This is a letter to your heart. You are moving quickly into sensitivity.

Sensing is awareness. Other faculties of your being are open to feel information. You are ready and willing.

This path you have chosen is more than you know. All who walk upon the earth are ready now for this change. The lesson is the growth of all your faculties.

You know this and you are ready to enjoy it and live within Christ. Stillness is always the guiding light. Appreciate this energy for it guides you to light.

*Be ready and willing
to go without restraint
The Light is your Path.*

In other worlds you have knowledge. Here you are learning emotion. In your heart you know the Christ Within follows emotion and leads with emotion into the spirit.

Everything you know is reversed. Listen to this statement and then feel it. Do not read it, but be nourished by the truth that you are the child of the heart. You are a Creator of light and you are light.

*Truth will set you Free
Truth is the Light that is not Seen
Truth is the Way
The Way is
Within*

You do not have to move to find the way or to move upon the way. You only have to imagine and you are there.

This is the secret. It is revealed by the removing of the struggle. Struggle is not happening, it is illusion, and illusion is seeing nothing.

Everything that is said, is said from a bias and bias is reality. This reality is made of time. Time is illusion.

The ego is time. When the ego is living there is time. You are made of time so your ego consciousness can exist. The reversal of time is what you are ready to undertake. Drive away confusion.

Allow the central theme that is easy to understand to be the one you follow. Avoid complexity. Reality moves from complexity to simplicity by pointing to something simple. The simple is positive.

It is the light and it requires the movement of feeling in order to reach it. Complexity is negative and makes feeling impossible.

*Feeling is your Soul Touching
Spirit and Knowing*

Gather all the Wisdom of the Tree of Life and Give it when you are ready to give it. This is the necessary step for you to know. Be ready to walk into the light.

*The Nature of the Christ Within
is to Lead with Pure Emotion
and to Know what is Right
for the Child of the
Heart to Learn*

BELOVED ~   ~ I AM

CHANGES

Telepathy is your communication of feeling through the higher mind. Christ speaks out in constant prayer to all who wish to shine out a beacon of light.

You are here to transmute the negative into positive. To move upward in the current toward greater insight. Allow this to happen. See your mind transform into invisible light.

The frequency of change is movement without sound, time without distance, speed without power, and mass without magnetic.

Mark the spiral of evolution in the center within and communicate feeling. Regenerate your words through your inner voice. Reverse your polarity.

*The Life Force Manifests
the Christ Within
Who Teaches You.
I Give you this Knowledge,
A Greater Arc of Truth moves
from Thought to Thought.
Ask, why is your Consciousness so
Preoccupied with the Past and the
future?*

Listen to your mind go from place to place and sense it is making every effort to get through the walls. Your thoughts bring you to alignment and give you a greater sense of yourself than you had before.

The nature of thoughts are like waves. They move in frequencies and in wavelengths. Thoughts move along a time pattern. A time pattern is an ego. Sense the nature of life with your truth respective of who you are now as an ego.

*Allow what you have learned
to be of value by being
of value to yourself.*

The small dream you have is one that is seen by many others in a constant reminder of Spirit.

There is lack in the world because humans seek that which they cannot have. Seeking separation rather than unity creates lack. Life which is unified cannot be broken to hold less than what it is.

When you ask for what is not truth, you are the only one who can experience this. You are brought into the measure of it and diminished into a smaller and smaller part of the whole.

You cannot be uncommitted, for you have asked for this commitment and to do anything less is to give away the power that you have worked so hard for. Seek to measure the nature of your experience.

*I am the Light of your Mind
and this is the Love
that is waiting
for you to Speak*

Be brought into the light and be made whole in it. I am in this truth, waiting for you to come into a new dimension and to bring it into the heart and soul of life itself. This is your new reality.

*I will Give you
Whatever you Ask

Ask for Love and
Ask it for All

Always Ask the Christ Within
for Oneness*

This is the nature of your birthright, for when you ask for what is held by every soul, every soul receives it.

BELOVED ~   ~ I AM

WORLD

By asking for less you are broken into pieces and fragments of personality by the law of action and reaction. It is with refraction you are splintered into many consciousnesses.

This forces a realignment in which you are brought back whole as you see the truth in others. This is the original form that must always be represented in the same manner, for it is coded by intelligence. It is the manifestation or the radiation coming from the Creator.

State with conviction, *"I Am God"*

Is this blasphemy and apostasy? The world has reversed the truth.

Apostasy is an impossible condition. It is not possible, and everyone realizes this when they are faced with the ludicrous task of redefining the role of God.

It is not for you to do this even if you could. You cannot know the ultimate reasons for they are beyond your grasp until you are unified and in one piece.

When you are in one piece you are in true alignment and in full consciousness. This means your eyes are vortexes of your soul, and they take others deeper and further into the mind of Source, and finally to the center of Spirit which is pure love.

I will call you when you are ready to hear the messages. Remember all life is sweet when it is mixed with love. This is the key for you to understand.

I will Guide You Now

You Are Coming Closer to the Heart Allow the Heart to Open In the Heart there is Stillness In this Stillness, I Am

I have listened to your words intermingle with your fears. Each time I was there when you needed me. I am here again now, to remove your fears and allow you to have what you wish for.

The reversal is the beginning of the resurrection. You may have this. Begin to understand the mysteries. Allow these mysteries to open your heart. To open means to allow the opening of your heart to be filled. Open and allow nourishment.

I have heard your calls for help over time. I have seen your light and your mind shine into the darkness and look for me. But you must know that I am not in the darkness. Look for light in the light. Look for joy in joy, and look for wisdom from the wise.

I Am here as your Servant to bring your Consciousness into the Heart of the Christ Within

Life is Equal, no Lesser or Greater All things are Possible

Beloved ~      ~ I Am

Child

pen your eyes and look to the ones who are wise & follow the spirit of truth. This is the Christ Within. It is your own self that holds the keys.

It is your own light that will guide you. No other follows the path you are on. I will guide you to the doorway, but you must cross the threshold and enter. You are the one that must follow the path. I am the one who calls you home.

I will Call without
Ceasing until your Return
I Am Awaiting
Within for your Return

You are experiencing the changing of your being as the world goes through its change. You find this happening whether you are conscious of it or not. This is the death that you fear, but it is not to be feared children. Have I not shown you that death is not something to be feared? It is but a moment from one place to another. I have shown you that you are not held down by fear.

Ask to be shown inside in a vision so that you may have this imprinted on your very being. I have done this and so you shall as well. This is the key, for you will unlock your own door.

Seek first The Kingdom of Heaven.
This is the first Truth I shall tell, to Trust!

Trust, is the correction you need. Allow joy and abundance in your heart. You are a child of the heart now become a child in Christ. This is your destiny.

There is another way, but it is long and dark and will take you away from me. It is to go outside your own being where there is nothing, where there is the expanse of sleep, and the tide that runs away from the light. This is the direction that will leave you without me, and so you will not be in my heart.

I can only Say you Have The Choice, I cannot Make it for you

I can only call and pray you see me in your heart, and come to me so we may fulfill the plan of love. The Source of All Creation wants this truth to be established and so I call out to you to return to this vision. This vision of love for all things to fit together in harmony. There is a purpose and a plan behind life.

You do not Remember our plan
This is part of the decision
You created Time so you
would think you were alone

This was to test your resolve for Love
To Understand Trust is
the Neighbor
of Truth

It does not matter if others question the truth of these words or the knowledge that you hold.

This is not the truth for you because you will find everything is in reverse. You may lack the patience to go on, but the road is sure and the destination assured.

Time Plays
no part in this
You have Already
Completed
the Journey
in this
Thought

Sananda

BELOVED ~   ~ I AM

BRIDGE

All your life you have worked to build a bridge back to your higher self. I Am the bridge. I Am Christ Within.

I hold the Door Open
Enter into the Kingdom

Your return is planned to be joyous. Celebrations are awaiting your acceptance.

Release what you hold onto here. Let the energy of your system return to God. Do not fear. You are well provided for. Safety is in your heart and nowhere else.

This is the Truth

You are not safe in this world without Christ. Without this love each moment you lose what you have. Do not fear, only enjoy and love. Right now, at this very moment, hold onto your emotions of love, and return to them only the highest.

If you could be released from this lesson, allowed to walk away now with nothing to leave behind and nothing to be concerned about, would you? If I were to lift you up into the highest places, now would you come with me? You may come with me in the highest places. It can be yours now. Allow it to be yours.

All is Protected
and Cared For
There is no pain
Allow the Light to Shine

You call out and ask again why does it seem so much of a struggle? And I say again, you do not know that the plan is freedom.

The plan has always been freedom, and so I am with you on this quest. The path is to express freedom and not struggle. I will not struggle. Know the joy of the Christ Within. Joy is not held, it is allowed.

I allow healing
light, energy & abundance
This is what I am
Made of and in every way

I am in the light
This is the light of my
Perfection, and so I am light
I can express it, and I believe it

I will walk with you and do what is called for by the plan so our lives are lived with freedom

I am the plan of love and light
In grace and perfect acceptance
in my heart is the child

I am the child who accepts Christ Within. I call out and answer I am ready and willing to follow the path of freedom

I am ready to fly. I am ready to lose myself and find myself

I am ready to trust your guidance and accept your vision as I walk with you into the light

I already know you and know that in your heart there is the goodness of the Infinite Creator that has brought all life to happiness. I know that you are in the love of the Creator who has made you.

In every way you are connected
to the central strand that
guides the path home

Quan Yin

BELOVED ~   ~ I AM

FOREVER

Forever follow the plan and the guidance of intelligence. It leads you home. You are closer than you know. In the stillness you have found Christ and in this stillness there is the heartbeat pointing to love.

I Bring You Within,
I Am Christ
I Will Guide You Home
I Guide You Home to
The Love of God, the
Source of All Creation
This is your legacy
This is the Truth

There is nothing for you to do but to accept and enjoy your life. This truth is your freedom. Allow yourself to move beyond the consciousness of time. Without time we are still one. Our path is without time and we move on the river of love.

Know this river moves without time through intelligence. Time is only an attribute of who you are. You are awareness of intelligence and consciousness of wisdom. This is the path of light.

Whenever you are full of love you are closer to the center of your soul where you are one with your own being and all beings. This is the path within.

The Christ Within guides you home. I am here to be that for you. I am the channel and expression of love so you may hear and you may see.

These words affect and alter your consciousness. This change is apparent in your attitude. Sense these words are inspired by the Christ Within.

I am forgiven in your eyes for I have forgiven the whole world. When there is a willingness to forgive the whole world for its errors then there is true willingness. In each soul is guidance.

Are you Ready to Become the Christ?

Speak from the heart of love and as part of the family of light. This is the simple reality of my story and life. I have forgiven the whole world, not part of it, not any one person, but everyone. There is not anyone that I have left out of this.

I Am the Way & the Light
for I Am Cleansed of All
Error for I have
Forgiven Everyone

Those who have not forgiven sit in judgment of others. In every judgment they obtain a mistake or sin that keeps them in the struggle and the turmoil of more lessons before they can learn to advance.

They will not advance until they have forgiveness. When the ones who go beyond are cleansed, they work within the world, helping to save the world.

Forgive Everyone
This is Your Peace
This is the Peace
of Christ Within

BELOVED ~      ~ I AM

ENERGY

ive in the energy given to us by the Creator. The Infinite Creator gives to us all we need. We are perfect. The path is to enlightenment. We have achieved peace.

*The Light of our being is not ours,
but the Creator's.
Feel light emanate through
your being with fulfillment and joy*

Live in the energy of love. Love is from the Infinite Creator and is part of every atom of our being. Know this feeling and experience it as perfectly as you breathe in energy.

*We are Perfect in our Own path,
the Path of Enlightenment*

*Live in the Light of Intelligence
and Illuminate Everything
you wish to learn
and understand*

I await you within Sanctuary

I await you as neither male nor female, neither old nor young, neither strong nor weak. You are within God. Each breath brings you closer.

Desires hold you away. They are neither permanent nor are they important. Think of the things that hold you away from Source and you will find nothing that is not already a part of Source.

Your family is part of Source and the pleasure of yourself can be completed by Source. Your needs are understood, but desires are appearances of things you do not need.

Within

Go beyond superficial feelings and aspirations that only cloud your real search. Your real search begins right now.

It begins with the words you hear. These words compel you to listen to the inner voice that speaks within you. I am within you and awaiting this recognition.

*Accept Love
face the Light
of the Spiritual
World Within*

Free your mind from the useless tantrums of greed, for the things of the material, emotional and mental worlds.

*I await your return in peace &
Know that your return will
Be Joyous and complete.*

It cannot be otherwise, for there is not time in our dimension to forestall this Destiny. I know you feel this Light and return to it.

*Expand with Light
go outward and
then Return with
Wisdom protected
by Love*

Archangel Michael

BELOVED ~   ~ I AM

TRUTH

Separation causes you to feel and believe in the pain, but it will not hold you, no matter how much pain you wish to endure.

Pain is self inflicted desire for that which is not possible. It is not possible to die, or to kill, or to be sick, or to be evil.

It is not possible to be alone, to be insane, to be worth less than another or to be unfairly treated. It is not possible because you are part of all that is and share the same eternal love of Source for all children.

We are One with Source and
this is the Divinity of Humanity
Oneness is the Essence of our being
Divinity Guarantees Love for All Eternity
There is nothing hurtful or shameful

All is Forgiven

You are not forsaken, nor abandoned. You are healed and feel this healing. It is wholeness not for you alone but for all.

Give the world your forgiveness. The world is your reflection. See in the world what you see inside your own being. I see what you see inside your own being. I see Love and wisdom in you.

Your Nature is Love & Wisdom
Express it through your Intelligence

There is no other Being than
The Infinite Creator
We Are All One

It is only time that keeps you from this realization. Time is a wall that you carry on the shoulders of your manifestation. It will pass as with the vibrations of your past and desires for experience. The path of your soul is homeward into love and wisdom. I breathe in and feel your return.

Your breath is inward as you evolve and return to center. It is not sad nor does it carry a loss of identity. Ascension is joy in finding identity.

This evolving is a simple realization of a being who knows itself as the Beloved I Am, fully conscious of its nature as infinite and eternal. It is beyond the comprehension of the concrete, logical mind.

Within the
Christ Consciousness
Experience this wholeness

Live your dream and take action
for your own evolution. Anything
contrary to your highest good will
only leave you in confusion and
sorrow. You are manifesting a
brighter and brighter light.

Bring Into

Manifestation

Christ Within

BELOVED ~   ~ I AM

Transformation

The feminine nature as intuition is reborn. Knowledge is pouring through the inner planes in potent and perfect ways. Your life is transforming quickly.

*New Souls are Being
Born With Higher
Telepathic Communication
Capacities*

Parents are teachers. Everyone is a parent and teacher. As a parent you are a steward. Honor your role. Give yourself time to develop this sacred trust and be able to give to the ageless children opportunities to release their gifts.

Incarnation is Healing

Dark forces and negative thoughts are crumbling. Global transformation is the power causing the release from negative thought forms. Millions upon millions of souls are incarnating for this purpose. Incarnation is healing. It is healing of thought forms.

Thought forms are Activated by personal desire. The energy must Pass out of them.

Dying out of personal desire can be very disturbing when not done from acceptance. Letting go is learned from the gentle and peaceful quality of the healers of love. Their empathy for humanity is dispassionately given.

*Deep experience and learning
is taking place
Humanity is Returning
Whole and Healed
You can Return Whole Again*

You have been able to deceive yourself into thinking that you are not of the Beloved I Am. Self-illusion and separation are powerful and still hold weight for you.

You have found the boundary within the illusion of desire for something which cannot be had. Desire always wishes for something it has but does not See.

*Desire for Eternal Life & Youth
 which you Have*

Desire for wealth which you Have

Desire for strength which you Have

Desire for Love which you Have

Desire for Wisdom which you Have

The denial Humanity purports is:

- There is no Divine,
    when the Divine is
    everywhere;
- There is not love,
    when Love is within
    all things;
- There is not security,
    when you are Within the
    Kingdom of Heaven at
    every moment;
- There is no truth,
    when you are always given
    what you ask for;
- There is no hope,
    when there is no need of
    hope for there is
  Understanding of the Divine Plan

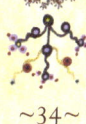

BELOVED ~      ~ I AM

CONCEPTION

nderstand the significance of your thoughts. Thoughts create harmonics. If the thought is pure and clean, it will bring the same to it. If it is too discordant, the next thought will be in discord.

The mind is an instrument, the same as a musical instrument. The mind operates in a myriad of rhythms and melodies.

find the Purpose to Provide
you with the Greatest
Expansion and Joy

The unconscious mind is always creating what you need to understand and travel through. It gives you the instant experiences to grow wiser, to show you where you need to turn.

Follow your insights. Continue on the sharp edged path of the disciple. Go into the light with the knowledge of thought and feeling. Life magically produces the results of your thought.

Purpose

Take hold of purpose, and put power into your life. You are a Cocreator. Make your life real. It is the image of your thoughts. It is the final hour before the change into the new dawn. The light from the rising sun is on the horizon.

*Awaken & Arise*
from the
Dream of Sleep
Go forward today

Be with others who are awake this morning. The change brings you the awareness of a grander plan. Leave behind the dreams of pain haunting your dark night of sleep.

Open
your Inner
Eyes to the Sun
See the Light of the world

It is not enough for you just to believe anymore. The grace you have is the Infinite's allowance for you to be a Cocreator. This is the awe-inspiring reality of which you are one with.

Time has no meaning,
yet there is Opportunity
There is Evolution in the
Infinite Universe of the
Beloved I AM

You are so much a part of it. You are the part that expresses and creates. You are the children of the Source of All Creation.

As children you grow. Your growth is directed by parents. The Christ Within guides your path. You are learning what judgment is. But as children, you are not aware of the world and are innocent. Become aware and know what is good for you.

You are pure of heart
and Keep this Heart Sacred
It is the birthplace of
the Christ Within

*Within the Stillness,*
Hear the Heartbeat
Know the Love
holding you Close

Paul the Venetian

Beloved ~   ~ I AM

Essence

Love is your essence. This essence is vibrant, intelligent and loving. Thoughts are the creation of mind. Love is the essence of mind.

The world needs healing to become righteous and sacred. The need for healing of bodies is also great, because the body is the display of thought and mind. Crime, illness and poverty are vividly displayed in your world.

The body is the sacred vessel of the soul and must be honored and understood. Your soul is not the problem; the problem is but a false idea, a situation. Let it go. Achieve righteousness by becoming healed. To have life abundant is to believe in healing.

See the Conscious
Evolution & Resurrection

The great purpose has many facets, colors and opportunities. You have much to offer back to universal being. Offer back health and healing in all the relationships you have within.

Consider the heart like the life of the flower that grows to express beauty. It is harmless and beautiful. It brings the essence of feeling and holds thoughts connected to the great system across the spaciousness of the universe.

What fruit shall you give?
Feel with every thought.
It is your bloom flowering
in response to universal light.
Feel the life force flow upward to express.

The mind is one and one with the Source of All Creation, but you exist as individual entities cocreating new life and learning, for Source allows the infinite.

Creation comes from the seed
As your seed is pure so shall
All of your Generations be Pure
Be cleansed and offer up perfection

Respond to the infinite with awe, wonder and sacred reverence. The infinite holds the energy of resurrection as its doorway into the greater life of spirit

Be cleansed of limitation. Find satisfaction, like the drop of water falling off a rock into a river's current. Be exposed once again to the family. There is no separation. Be within the river flowing to the ocean. Be reborn into the unmanifested oneness of eternity.

forgiveness

Forgive & forget the path of your daily activities. For a moment, understand the nature of what you are. You exist as one among a collection of souls working in unison and interconnected synthesis.

Your mind is the same in every aspect to all minds and all Love. You contain the same love. When you give love out, it returns. It is the pervading essence and core of all life, and love is expressed through the mind. Unfold love to the earth and to humanity.

Bring peace into the realm of your mind
Cleanse the images of your world
in whatever way is open, heal
the world you are part of

BELOVED ~  ~ I AM

LIFE

Exquisite fragrances of divine spiritual life open the doors to a new day disclosing a new vision. The sweet smell of the fragrance of life opens the door to a new light shining in from your heart

You know about the world you live in. The outer world is caught in illusions. Walk away from illusions. You ask about finances, land masses, storms, the material things you want on the physical level, but what is that?

In the physical world, you concern yourself with the phenomena, raging storms, war, poverty, crime. But focusing on these does not bring you closer to truthful answers.

What Makes Sense to You?

Is it something that will last for you?

You will be forgiven for what you have done and there is nothing that you can do that will be significant in destruction and regeneration. Nature will walk over your physical treasures. There is nothing lasting in the physical world.

In the Spiritual Life

Our Teacher walks with Source

The Infinite Creator

In Intelligence and Love

The Teacher brings the lesson

The lesson must be learned.

You believe the practical side of life knows nothing of this teacher. In this practical life, you have the belief of pain and loss. Nothing survives Time.

Nothing in your world can exist beyond your thoughts. You are the creator of the lesson. The teachers require you to learn it.

Beyond your Highest Realization

you will Learn that you are to accept the

Mantle of Power from the Christ Within

Do not block your Acceptance of Power

Ask for grace, ask for the power to let go. You are holding on, and Christ cannot take away your grasp if this is what you want.

I offer to you the same as I have received, wisdom to let go, and to let the Source of All Creation guide you. This gives you the power to channel the wisdom of Christ Consciousness.

Live, Move and Breathe in Spiritual Reality

This is the Nature you Wish in Secret

In the World you have evaded your greatest Wish

Ask for what you have Come here to Do

When you are ready to Ask

Request to Become a

Channel for the Christ

This is not hard. Wish to follow in the footsteps of the teacher. Learn who you are. Be the archetype of humanity. Be the clear channel.

Do you believe this is arrogant or that you are being foolish? These are deceptions and evasions. Decide to let go of resistance and struggle.

Christ is not difficult or Mysterious

"I Am"

Radiant Vital

Energy of Righteous

Creative Spiritual Life

BELOVED ~   ~ I AM

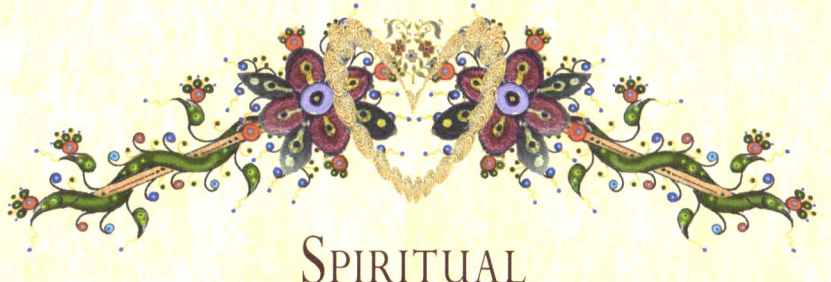

Spiritual

peak in the voice of eternal love. You have every right and privilege. Bring forth the power of Source. You are a Cocreator.

Christ Within
Brings Truth

Truth will allow no substitute. This power is yours to bring unity. This power the BELOVED I AM has granted you cannot be changed.

this Power is Love

Illusions, pain, suffering, and shame are created in your mind when ordered by you. The veil covers up the love of the Beloved I AM Presence from your eyes when you move away from this reality and the principles of God. See illusions and see the truth. When you are one with the Infinite Creator then you may say:

 I am the Truth
the Way
and the Life

The way the Divine is, you are. Utilize your creative powers and follow along the line of truth and life. Your life is made whole and clear.

The power of the Holy Spirit is the action of the mind of the Infinite Creator. This river of spiritual energy flows to righteousness.

You are made in the image of eternal love to be a cocreator. You are in error or sin when you are living in illusion and believing it is reality. Only you can see this illusion. Error is revealed by those of like mind.

Respect the power of Eternal Love

Here is where your adventure is lost, for you still feel that you must own, control and possess. This grasp of materialism holds back your vision and you do not see the value of ideas that go far beyond all of this.

A Channel of Christ
Knows this world must
be brought to the
Understanding of what it is

You are a child on a small planet
who needs to be awakened from sleep

There is a Call from the
Beloved I AM to Awaken

You are dreaming a dream that is unkind and does not fit his kingdom. Your home is filled with happiness and truth.

The personality has no power. It is weak in the spiritual realm and seems strong in the physical. There is nothing in the physical that you can have and keep.

The body grows old and dies. Food rots if it is not digested. Your air becomes polluted without nature's assistance. There is nothing in the world you can have. It is all meaningless without the life of the Spiritual.

All Revelation is Spiritual.
Are you ready to be a
Channel of the Christ?

The spiritual Life grows like a Tree in the soil of the Earth. The Tree does not own the soil, or the Light, the rain, the air, and the creation of its Life. The Tree grows in harmony according to its creator's wishes and respects its seed.

Rowena

BELOVED ~  ~ I AM

Realize

Let go of your intellectual force and let the spiritual life become your nature. Why must you fear realization from within your heart?

*Who would hold you back
from being like Christ?*

*Be like Christ and you
become Powerful*

Without Christ you are a dying physical personality faced with desires and pains. Do you think it is arrogant to be like the Infinite Creator? By saying this you say that Christ is arrogant, and make the Creator a monster. If it is arrogant, then no one would love or wish to be like the Creator.

*Be the Energy of Eternal Love
Be whole in
Greatness & Perfection*

Why would anyone avoid Being like the Divine? What do you hold against Christ? Divinity does not punish nor make life to be of pain. It is not like that at all. If you were Source, would you punish? If you would, then who would
you be?

*Look into your Heart
Release fear
fOLLOW THE Path*

Given You to Heal to forgive
This is the Path of the Light
Shine into all Places of darkness
Renew Life where it has Grown dim
Bring the fire into the Center
So All May Share Again its Warmth

Life requires you to Speak

As a channel of Christ, you are here to reveal the word and reveal heaven on earth. The lesson is not that you have grown evil, but that you are not willing to accept The power that is given, because of your desire to stay lost.

Do you wish to stay lost?

All who are walking upon the path know they are on it. You know you are lost and see the illusion of personality. You see the way each Life is faced with problems and dilemmas.

Why are people in your Life?

What Do they Bring you?

They bring you change so you can break free from the hold of fear. They force you to let problems die and become the holy grail.

When you are ready and empty, receive the spirit of the Divine. Become & accept within the power of Christ. Realize each person is made of divine light of Christ. In each person know this divinity. They hold you in the same manner of love.

*In all things is
The Beloved I AM*

Realize in each Moment
YOU ARE
Asked to See Oneness

In each Moment
Realize where Source is
and where Source is not

Realize this and you will find

Christ Within

Sanat Kumara

BELOVED ~ 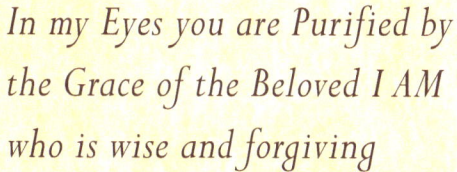 ~ I AM

Awaken

Mother Earth awakens & brings eternal love back into her home. She has slept and is with child, which is you, and you are in labor of birth.

New energies and new times are changing your world. Truth lives on this earth and it is being born & awakened through you. This is your dimension.

Open up to a greater understanding of what and who you are. Yours is the power to live in full conscious life. Yours is the power to let go of pain.

You have walked the path of fear. Fear is always there until you realize you are creating fear in order to be separate from becoming a channel of Christ.

As a channel of Christ you give up the fear, anger, and hatred. You accept and forgive all of humanity, and not only those whom you care for.

All Deserve, Receive Forgiveness

I have forgiven all the untold billions upon billions who have strayed from Truth and gone into the path of pain. I have forgiven each and every transgression against you, and have forgiven you of your sins, your transgressions, for what you have done, and for what you have failed to do.

I forgive those who are victims, who allow their power to be lessened by others, and for not accepting spiritual power. I forgive those who walk the dark path of control and abuse.

When they Choose to Accept the Light, I forgive them. The Law Brings them back to Truth. I have forgiven the weak who have not Accepted the Light because of a lack of faith in The Source of All Creation When they Choose the Light, they are healed

In my Eyes you are Purified by the Grace of the Beloved I AM who is wise and forgiving

No one wishes to be in anger, pain & revenge or evil you know is wrong. Call out for your own healing. Why is the alcoholic who is lost in his own misery condemned for the pain that he endures?

Why are many of the children lashing out in violence without respect for life? They do not have guides, no one to be a Wayshower and bring them the light of the future. Become the channel of Christ Within and show by your example, and lead the path home.

There is no darkness when you are a Channel of Christ Light You are Within The Family of Light

I will speak for you. I will settle your score & you are forgiven. I have forgiven you as I am forgiven. This is grace of the loving Infinite Creator. You are given power, love and peace.

Is it that you feel unworthy to finally be what you have intended in your secret thoughts? When you are brought into the light do not hide it. The light shines, and you are always seen, and your deeds are judged as worthy.

You are always Loved and you are never alone Please take my hand

Mother Mary

Beloved ~ ~ I AM

Light

In the light, feel your soul give you the right to be. Awaken in a lift of spirit. See in a new way, a perfect vision past time, and enter into a new awareness.

In each Heart
there is a Center and all are
Searching for Center

In the Quiet of the Soul
there is the Center that Awakens

Let down your barriers and open up. Be what you are. Be willing to let it happen. Find the center and find peace. I am here to bring you into the center.

Lift up your Head
Allow Light to Enter
Let Light Lift you Upwards

In other times you know of, there has never been peace. There have been different dreams, but never peace.

Peace stays and endures. You are here because you have not truly desired peace. You find conflict to suit your purposes. What is your purpose? What is your motive?

 Desire

Desire for conflict brings violence, perpetuates rage, and leaves no room for gratitude. You are not grateful for pain. You cannot be. The soul does not know of pain.

There is no one who would desire rage over peace, hate over love, and fear over wisdom. But this is what you create in ignorance and darkness.

Intend to Make

Love Happen

Let me speak freely to you, and all who like you, wait at the doorstep. Cross the threshold and enter, for you are lost, more than those in the wilderness who are seeking and finding struggle.

You understand peace and know where your heart is, yet you wait at the threshold. Let your whole being enter, for you are sure of the outcome. Hear the music inside the temple.

There is Peace, happiness
and the Enlightenment
of your Soul waiting
for you Within

This is the Truth
This is the Way

I am here to lead you as your guide our eyes are covered with tears and struggle, but yet you wait. Walk the footsteps of all who have traveled the quest.

You know the way to the initiation and have come too far to stop at the moment when you are upon the threshold. It is for all of humanity, not just for you.

You Are

not alone

in the Light

BELOVED ~   ~ I AM

VOICE

Again I hear in your heart: "I do not wish for Christ to control me." It is not Jesus that comes into your heart, but rather the power of Christ Consciousness. Jesus is within Christ, but not Christ. The Jesus personality is pure, true, in wholeness & acceptance.

The Christ Consciousness is centered in the teacher, guided by the will of the Father. Respect and use this power for healing and for truth.

*Christ speaks
in many ways
with many Voices
The Way is Within*

Christ expresses truth and divine life. His fruits are pure and sweet. Christ abides always in righteousness. In the clear, pure heart Christ consciousness lives within, he is like a pearl.

*Christ Manifests Spiritual Power and
the Creative Will of the Combined force
of the Divine Father & Mother Energy*

*Christ is the Truth and Sees
Goodness in you*

In Seeking the Better Way,

*you have Always looked to be
like the Divine Beloved I AM*

As a child of the Infinite Creator, you have sought this in selfishness. Still in this direction, you looked at your path, always seeking to have more, be more.

Your way may be filled with obstacles, yet still you have sought to have more, and be more. Your way might have focused on the physical level, wanting sensuality and pleasure, but it was still to be more, to be better.

In losing the favor of your higher self, the ego or devil, has led you to temptation so that you might be tempted. Refuse this false path.

The path to Christ lifts your spirit from selfish concerns and lifts you from inertia into action. You know you have always sought for the highest in the way you thought was best. You have fought for self interest because this is the way you were taught.

*I am with you to guide and
teach you a new way
I will not allow you to forget
Wisdom and Love
The Way of your World
is Love and Wisdom*

Take love with you wherever you go and you will never be without a light to guide your path, and to guide those whom you care for. Care for all. In my open heart is the center.

*The Center
is Opening*

It grows wider the more it opens to you, and so I open it more and more. I receive more and more love the more I give to you. It fills me with the divine pleasure the Infinite Creator wants for all of us.

*I Am One with you so
I may open the power
within each of you
Spiral up through
The Great Center
of Our Heart*

~50~

BELOVED ~   ~ I AM

Hear

Something within you calls your name and says

"Come with Me"

And I do surely call, and I listen for your reply for I have ears to hear the things of the Spirit. I hear this soft reply, and I know it calls me to listen, and come to your side.

*There is another call for you,
and I Hear it now
I am pleased by others,
for this is a gift of Love
Receive this gift and let it go to
your very center and continue
long after all thoughts are gone*

*Be more than your thoughts
Intuitively feel this Awareness*

When you please the one who is your neighbor, you are bringing yourself to center, allowing Source to reach out and touch others through you.

This gives you the power of the Holy Spirit to breathe in the life of the I AM presence. This is the greatest of loves, and the unifying power of the holy relationship.

*Face this life in a new way
Face it with power
and courage to
say the truth*

The truth speaks so loudly it does not have to be spoken with force. The truth has depth, and it will bring this power to the heart like no other force can.

*Speak the
Voice of Truth
Live the Life of Play
Journey into the Mind
Understand the Divine
Take Time to be in Silence
Always be very Grateful
Hear the Sound of Soul*

Let Go

Enlighten Humanity

Be Harmless Be Honest

Live Prosperous

Enjoy Truth

Give Forgiveness

Be Creative

Love God with

All Your Heart

BELOVED ~   ~ I AM

The Gift

The word truth is the way of your soul. Enter the kingdom. You want more power. You want to know a powerful truth that will move you off the doorstep and into the kingdom.

This is the Truth

You are not in any way Powerful
You are not Courageous
You are not Loving
You have none of these attributes
Outside of the Kingdom

This is the Truth

You have nothing until you enter the Kingdom with willingness. Let go of the false pride that makes you want to keep gaining knowledge of things. This is not important until you come into the Kingdom & find yourself

Accept and Forgive Yourself for Dreaming a False Reality

Reality is not what you manufacture on the astral plane of desires, or in the fanciful ideas inherent in the volumes of thoughts pervading the galaxies. Reality is the power in you to be a channel of Christ.

This power is yours, and it is yours always. Accept your power willingly, and accept it fully. Make the plan real, to be understood by all.

This is Power

The theme of your Life is when? When will you let go of the world that holds no value? When will you fulfill your promise? You are the Promise of Eternal Love, the Promise of the Divine to do Good.

The Will of the Infinite Creator is to do Good and You are this Promise.

In Acceptance

Upon the altar I accept to go into the night and bring the candle of wisdom. To lead my brothers and sisters to the kingdom. It is made in the divine image holding presence in silence.

I hear a painful cry in the wilderness. I know this is the shroud of a soul lost to knowledge of this kingdom. The gift of life gives us life forever replenished, like the fountains of water springing up through the earth.

I am unlimited light and abundant energy. Light flows up through my feet and down through my eyes and meets in the center of my being to form a star.

I AM this Star that radiates out to you and brings you inward with the magnetism of wisdom and the attraction of love. The gift of life is given with pleasure, wisdom and the love of the Source of all Creation.

At the Threshold

If I could give you a special gift this day it would be to say how special this very moment is. Listen and hear only the sound of silence. Listen for the peace of soundlessness.

Hear peace in every thought and know love in every moment of silence. The music of silence knows only rapture. Words lose their touch when the gift is life.

*Grace is in every Instant
I Am, so I Am,
I Am the Christ Within*

BELOVED ~      ~ I AM

REVELATION

**D**ream of what you are
Your body is of light. Your mind is full of wisdom. Why is this hard for you to accept? Let the awareness you have open up.

Remember

In your Mind is a Spark as each Star is in the Heavens. There are more Stars in the Skies than there are Humans

In every Star is a Celestial Being
Guiding you and holding onto
Love for you.
You are never forgotten.

You are always Loved & always cared for

The Family of Light stretches across the galaxy. They are your brothers and sisters from each star, from each light, and they are here to be with you forever.

You have forgotten as you have played out the dream to Incarnate. You are admired for the work that you are doing.

Please do not let the time slip past this moment. I am here to take you back into another world, a higher dimension you have been away from. It is empty without you and you are not at peace until you return to your center and come home.

In your life you are and have much. When I look into your heart I see the radiance of light. I do not have to convince you of this for this you know.

The earth loves you. She gives you life. She is your home and you live with her. Lead your brothers and sisters out of the darkness. Darkness has been created by your shadow. She can no longer contain the pain you hold on to.

She KNOWS you are not Living in your Light.
She is giving you the chance to find your way back. The time has come for you to return home.

Accept the Gift

The Gift will bring you back

The gift is Simple

for some and hard for others
Let yours be whatever it takes
to Bring you Home

Accept it and know I will be there for you and bring you home into the light. There is a greater reality than the one you see. Whatever the method, know it has been planned.

Earth is a
Beautiful Being
that Shines with
Wisdom and Mercy

She has given you the place to
Live

She has afforded you time,
but the time is now over for you
must come home and be part of

The Family of Light

Accept the Gift

and hold onto it

for it is Precious

Arcturus

Beloved ~   ~ I AM

Home

Creation is not what you have created. It already is and always has been. Creation is for you to enjoy and be a part of. You are searching and this tells you that you are lost.

The fact that you ask the question gives you the knowledge to ask for answers. The question of life is the key. In all of this, still you fail to see death and pain are not real. Life is all there is.

Symmetry

The awareness of your Immortality is encoded in every Cell of your Body
The timelessness of your Life is the function of your Mind

The higher mind thinks within a timeless matrix. It cannot be explained away by the formulations of the lower mind. The concrete and rational body of reasoning is nothing but collections of facts on a limited scale of perception. They only have validity on a small scale and are useless to your search.

A higher frequency of vibration is changing the structure of your world. This change is happening at an increasing acceleration. Atoms vibrate between the cells of your body. Particles gather around its nucleus. All have consciousness.

There is a duality of light and dark.
All Duality in Nature is fused within Love

Duality is the way things are. This is not danger. Danger is ignorance and fear. Fear is created to keep you away from love.

Love dissolves fear. Light dispels darkness. Your mind has been limited to a sphere on the third dimension. Your consciousness is being opened to other possibilities. Life is much more than a short life on a planet filled with tragedy and death. This is not your existence.

Truth sets you free

The Universe is Alive with Consciousness. Life is not limited to the Earth. Be a mirror to those who are in need of your clarity to see light. Life is a bigger picture. It is not about the money or power anymore.

Life is about Truth & Love Here within your Heart

Your existence is multi-dimensional. This is logical. You are consciousness. The nature of consciousness is based on a life of intelligence of the Creator. Universal law requires all things to be representations of the parents.

The apple tree does not produce pine cones and so on and so on. The apple seed does not limit the apple tree to being less or different than it itself is. This is the nature of the law of creation.

Beloved ~  ~ I AM

Reflection

ace yourself. See your etheric double in your reflection. See the vibration of spiritual impulses. Understand the other side.

See how the material self can be a block as it resists the power of spiritual emanations. Understand how you might begin to perceive how the thoughts you are feeling right now are of no value to you.

The thoughts I am speaking of are the unsaid rejections of yourself. The rejection of my words that say you are the Son of the Infinite Creator, the daughter of the Infinite Creator, and you are divine.

The rejection of the inner voice is not only yours, but is portrayed through you by the impersonations of your life in your relationships, with television, movies, books, schools, neighbors, towns and the countries of your world.

Each time you see the rejection of the voice of Christ it is a replay of your own thought, no one else's but your own. This is how much power you have in your world. Your world is shaped by your thoughts and reflects how you are compatible with it.

I am your
Higher Self
Watching over you
like a Star in the Sky

You do not Know
what you do in this form

Resurrection Gives
Life to this form

It becomes the Servant
of the Christ Within.

There is forgiveness in
Compassion & Understanding

Call

I speak to you through your illusion

The veil is thin. A part of you knows me without a doubt, but then on the other side of the veil, you cannot see me at all. I am with you always and there is greatness in you. I am always there to forgive you for not seeing and knowing.

There is nothing you can do that I will not forgive. You must know I am forever forgiving you for what you know not of. Hold to me and listen. I forgive what you will not. Until you accept forgiveness, there is nothing. You command your own destiny.

With all of my effort, love, and even with the grace of all my powers, I cannot release you to life unless you ask.

I am the Power to grant your
every wish and to Guide
you into the Light, if you ask.

I hear your call across the universe. Across time I am here at the instant you ask and in that moment of asking. I will give you what you wish for.

In that Moment
Peace will Be yours
All you must do is ask
Ask is the last word of the Omega
In the World of the Omega,
Last is Peace

When you find me
you will know peace

BELOVED ~   ~ I AM

Asking

I am in you and with you at every moment. This is unity. I speak always within you as easily as you are reading or hearing these words.

It is Given to me to be your Guide

Who is to say what my name is other than I Am that I Am? These words are for you to hear. They are truth and answer your need. I can tell you that you are finished and have accomplished your destiny. Still the world will say, "stay and face this, or face that difficulty, and overcome this, or overcome that because you are not finished."

I say that you are finished with this world. In this world you are never alone for I am by your side and bring you into the Light.

A Great Light is in your Mind
it is always Being given
This is the Truth of Love
It is Given so you can Open
Into your Light

Do not believe the Beloved does not love you as much as another, or suffering is a virtue. Do not ask to suffer, or believe you wish to cause pain. Pain is always self-inflicted, but it becomes the pain of the world. This is the nature of your pain. Your wish to survive pain is not that you want to live with it, but that you struggle rather than create.

Creation is your gift
you are the One
who consecrates
with God

When you are part of the Light,
then you have what the Family has.
Then you have Unlimited Power
to do the things that are
of Principle and of Divinity.

There is nothing
to do other than
To Ask,
to Ask and Ask again
until you Believe and
Know what you are
Asking for
In the last Days Time Will cease

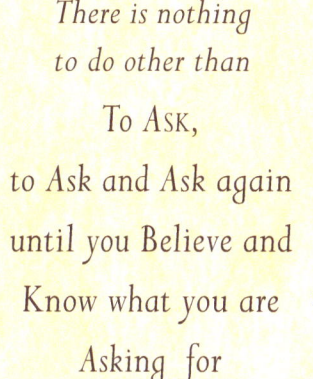

The Greatest Light is shown by the One who Opens the Door. The door is Opened by the humblest and the One who Asks to Be in the Presence of the Eternal.

Please Ask

There can be no stipulations put on this final request of the omega. It is the final play and the final act.

You must be ready to ask for release, to be released from the desire to live in darkness. There is no sadness. You may think you have to be punished for living away from truth, that you are guilty and should be ashamed. But no, you are forgiven.

You are always forgiven. Listen again. You are forgiven. There is nothing about yourself that you need to be ashamed of. You are divine in every way, if you would see your light as I do, you would be fulfilled in truth.

You Are
the Divine Light
Shining in the Sky
like a Star

BELOVED ~  OPEN  ~ I AM

**A**sk for your Acceptance, neither to control the world of God, nor to be a servant.

Do not ask to be in the light and be powerful as an example of this greatness, but ask to be there for only the love of The Creator.

 ## To Rest and to find Peace,

To be home within family, to know you are loved and valued is within your birthright. You were born and you were wanted by the Beloved I AM. In every instance, you are the one the Infinite Creator loves.

Please ask for this desire. My greatest desire is for you to have yours. By having your wish, it brings you joy. Your smile brings the greatest gift, knowing the Eternal Loves.

I am not fulfilled by your pain, your poverty, your lack or your ignorance. This does not give joy. I know you as you do not know yourself. You see the pain. I do not.

There is a glory inside of you that you must ask for. If I could ask for you I would, but then your life would be gone. You must ask to be what your ultimate calling has made you for.

I ask to be what my Ultimate

Calling has made me for

I ask it Now &

I ask it Again

I know I will receive what the Source of All Creation has made me for, has fashioned my heart and mind to do, and what I have been given to create with.

I ask to be able to

Serve the Divine

I ask to be Joyous in the Way Eternal Oneness Made Me

I ask any and all of Eternal Love's highest angels to give me powers to do what Source has made me for.

I ask to be the one Source made me to be. I will follow and seek the highest good at all times and listen to my heart as it teaches me what the Divine has made me for.

I know I did not make myself and that I am a Divine child of the Beloved I AM. And Source has a purpose for me to understand my heart and express it in my life. There is love within and there is joy for eternity.

I ask to receive the life and abundance the Divine I AM made me for

I hear you reject part of it in asking, "why would Source design such a life for me?" It is because the One is good and the I AM Presence wants only good for you. Do not think that the Divine does not want your good. This is the only thing your Infinite Creator wants for you, to be a shining light on your path.

Understand…

You travel the lighted pathway so you may find exactly what would serve you and the ones you are with. There is no pain or difficult time in this. It is neither hard to understand, nor too difficult a path.

You are being guided
as fast as you can
Release the weight
& Rise higher

There is no need to be afraid of this journey, for there is something here you know very well, and this is who you really are.

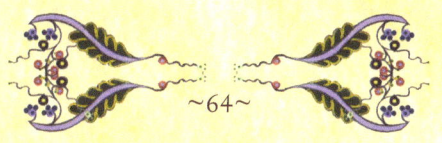

Uriel

BELOVED ~   ~ I AM

Accept

Asking what the Infinite Creator made you for is the first step. The next step is accepting what the Creator made you for. When you accept this path, then you are ready for inheritance.

You may have all
that the Creator is in your life
when you Accept what you were made for

Do not ask why. Acceptance is not about asking why. It is about accepting what you are. It is about owning you are worthy. The power and your relationship to it, is true.

In the River of Life,
Love is the Current
In this River you are washed
Clean with Forgiveness

There is no shame, no lack, no sin and no judgment. You are whole and free to be part of the new world. Say with me, "I accept what Eternal Oneness has made me for." Now say, "I will do what the Beloved I am has made me for."

I not only Ask, but I will do, and

I am doing what Source made me for

I have not strayed from The Path, but

I have not known where I was

I was lost, and Now

I Am found

Life

I am what the Eternal
Created me to be
Beloved I Am worthy of Love
I have Asked and I Know the Source
Of ALL Creation Made Me to Love

The Infinite Creator made me and loves me, and now, with love in my heart, I am doing what I was made for. I am doing what the Infinite wanted me to do. I am to create, to create what I truly want, joy and happiness.

My happiness is continual and eternal. I live in the light of oneness, and know I am in the vision of my being, whole, and complete and at peace. There is nothing I need to do.

I Am Open
to The Divine's
Love for me

I know I am taken care of. If I am alone and caught in stagnation, without the hope of love, then I Am lost, and being lost, I must be found at some time.

Search and call out
Ask for help
The Time has come to See
The Light of Wisdom and say,
"please find me"
Show me the way to reach
out of the darkness
and enter into The Light.

Jophiel

BELOVED ~   ~ I AM

Feeling

nter into the silence and find your Soul waiting to lead you on in the ways of Spirit. This is power. Power comes and binds you in Spirit.

Spirit is the feeling of Soul that provides Joy and release from form

The creative ray of life separates itself into the multitudes to create manifestation of diversity. Life brings about the infinity of variation.

Life is complete and eternal. Its colors change in dazzling arrays of mathematical intelligent formulations that are beautiful and artistic.

The Wonder to Understand is feeling

Feeling is the continuous reorientation of the direction, intensities, quantities and qualities of the rays. They blend and transform each other in a planned and principled interchanging relationship.

Personality

Let go of personality and walk on a beam of light. Face the light and move through it and follow it upward. Meet your Soul and become aligned with its purposes.

The Soul arrives quietly and with great strength as it takes over the personality. The personality does not willingly allow this to happen.

The personality will never have peace until the Soul takes upon itself the life created for its Benefit.

The personality feels the pull of the Soul. It knows the power of its greater being. When it lets loose of the reins of time, the Soul reclaims the emotions and feelings.

The Soul is the power of spirit and the heart of eternal love. If I am lost, I will ask for help.

The BELOVED I AM will show me where I am and how I can find my way home. In my heart I hear the call to know this is my home. To know I am in truth and working with divine intelligence.

I Create with the Divine according to its Principles In this I know that I am Inspired

The Divine I AM presence does not need servants. The Divine needs its family whole and complete where all are loved with equal measure. Feel the power of eternal oneness in every moment. Know the greater plan.

I am here to Set the Course of Life A Course to Surmount the Self of the World and follow the Spirit and Soul, the Christ Within

The self of the world sees limitations, dangers, fears, and worries, but the soul will guide you on and upward into the light of consciousness.

Let the lower self know the Will of the Soul The Will of the Soul Guides you to Peace

Beloved ~   ~ I AM

Transition

The Soul is much more than the personality. The personality only knows itself through sensory knowledge. It is the primal mental awareness in the lower mind.

The higher body of the Soul must allow transition to be one of alignment. This is the necessary change.

*Soul is taking Over and
giving the personality peace
for it has done its work*

The personality experienced form as individuated learning from the material world in time & space and sees itself in specific and particular lives.

The time frame mechanism made it appear it was living as a separate being, but the higher mind was not fooled nor affected by any of the disturbances in this time frame. Time frames mean nothing for they have no existence outside the personality experience.

*Soul is aware of Cycles of
Evolvement and has planned
this for its own Experience
The Soul has a Plan that
IS directed through the
Spiritual Will*

Soul is looking to grow, evolve, to experience and to create with more variation, power and intelligence. The plan of transition has a mental, spiritual, emotional and physical path.

Intention

The interrelationship of all the other characteristics of life make life complete. There is polarization in life. The In breath of involution is the learning. The out breath is the externalization of knowledge.

The Creative force Seeks Expression and Experience

The creative force moves across the waters of the unmanifested to manifest and create life in different and continually interesting ways. The intention of life is to be ever variant and growing while ever centralized and learning.

The basis of the Universe is Intelligent Love

*Love with Intelligence is the
Will to Good which Manifests
More Good and More Knowledge.
When Words are Spoken,
Language falls short upon the
ears of sensory Humanity*

The first Plan
The Path of Life
IS Creation

*The creation becomes what
it was created from, and this
creative force walks through
the universe at all the levels
of consciousness, for this is
the basis of life.*

Beloved ~  ~ I Am

Experience

The universe is consciousness. There is nothing which does not contain consciousness. Consciousness is the basic and undivided principle of existence. Love & wisdom are synonymous parts of the creation of the Beloved I Am.

*With Intelligence
all things are willed into being*

The life of divine love is the life of humanity. This is the nature of the Eternal's existence, to be what humanity thinks it is not. The paradox of this is so often repeated. Humanity feels unworthy because humanity is confused as to what it is.

*Infinity is the representation
of the Creator's Mind.*

The universe is your body, and love is the binding force that holds it all together.

It is as simple as this. If for no other reason than to live & breathe, you exist. A purpose greater than this is your goal. This greater purpose is to express eternal oneness as it cannot become manifest as you are.

Why is it that you confuse the reality of this transformation? See the illusion of pain and sacrifice as the negation of soul, and you will see it cannot be real and everlasting.

The higher mind is accessible, ever ready to give and receive. It is not directed by the conscious or subconscious mind, it simply is. Do not agree with illusions distilled from extraneous and divergent thoughts. Do not forget who you are.

You are Divine

Divine means you are ineffable and beyond comprehension. You are an undivided unity. Divine in an individual manifest form. Source is essence, creator, the unmanifested being.

DIVINE BELOVED I AM

You are of the divine Beloved's essence and this essence is infinite. Life is expansion. Breathe peace inward and breathe light outward. Find within your mind the inward returning to the center which is the in-breath. Breathe out infinite variety and limitless love

The mind held in the receptacle of bodies is so distant from the truth that it holds no thought of its origin. This is the nature of your dilemma. You cannot conceive of the universe without grappling with its infinite dimension.

You cannot cope with the thought of time without facing the concept of eternity. Your present consciousness is infinitesimal in relation to eternity. You cannot fathom emotions without knowing they are unending, with depth beyond the receptacle of the human heart.

*In a Moment
of Silence
Think of an end*

The lower mind loses itself in awe and disbelief. The ego of each person is strong and keeps this illusion alive for no other reason than to create the illusion of pain and suffering, cherishing its false treasures.

It is impossible to think of an end. In death you will see no end, but a renewal of life.

The Moment of death is a Release

Each Moment of Life is Joyous

Michael

BELOVED ~   ~ I AM

Communion

Why the world? Why is it poverty of the spirit is being unquestioned? Why do a fortunate few see the long distance, hear the inner words. Why is it for them to face alone the questions That leave others shuddering in the night?

The children of the world see into the night sky and hear the thunder and see the lightning.

Is the power of the Infinite Creator as distant to them as the rambling sound of thunder in the distance? Or is it right within their hearts, waiting to unfold? Death, in true form, is release of spirit and life. The ego is the chaining of the spirit to the body. Ego chooses to judge. When the body is chosen over spirit, life becomes cold, leaving your soul without purpose in the world.

Let go, let go of the things that bind you to the earth. Find freedom from your ego. The ego has a strong hold on all who wish to have that which they cannot, separation in a body.

At the root of all things

...the ego wants separation
Spirit always wants Unity

The ego wants separation so it can blame, cause disagreement, feel superior, create resentment, be in anger and attempt to control time. What the ego cannot have is immortality. The ego is the lower mind that judges, chooses, and becomes conscious with the body. It only exists inside this sphere or time cell. This is all humanity knows thus far.

If the ego is to find deeper knowledge, it must relinquish its hold on the mind and body, and become infused with Spirit. The ego is also called the personality.

It is like a child growing up, playing childish games and learning through experience. Why did it happen that the ego became sentient and the Spirit remained dormant? How can the Infinite fit into a bottle?

The Transmutation of the mind into lower forms necessitates the introduction of a vehicle to understand the lower levels of existence.

See Beyond

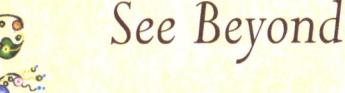

The Source of All Creation is Complete

In completeness, there is Perfection

In the perfection there is Expansion

In expansion there is Growth

In growth there is Learning

In learning there is Wisdom

In wisdom there is Love

Love pulls everything along. In all of this love there is the will of intelligence. The will of intelligence is taking all of humanity on a higher loop and a broader scale of life

The past and the future are mental concepts. Now is the only reality. There is infinity of now moments extending outward, backward, forward, beyond and within each mind.

This Now is the Realm of the
BELOVED I AM Presence

Your Moment is Now,
and for you a Memory.

I hold this thought you have within the grasp of your attention. Think for a moment within yourself about who you are and how you feel.

Desire
Spiritual
Emotion Now

BELOVED ~   ~ I AM

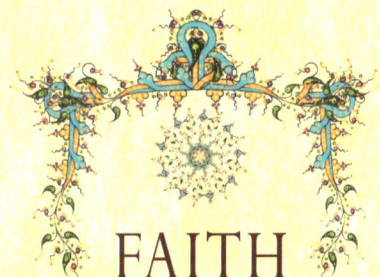

FAITH

Faith is to perceive as The Eternal Creator does. Faith to know the perfection of all things. Faith to understand the timing of reality.

The knowing of how and why things work out is the power of the will aligned with perfect knowledge. Only the life caught in illusion suffers the pains of the false rule of an ego that makes unhappiness a virtue and loneliness a standard.

See beauty and the expanse of life open up before you forever and ever. Create a sacred monument of the now and unfold it into life.

You are faced with the dilemma of how to survive in a world that is false to the core. The falsity of it makes you feel the value of your own being as fake. This negative interchange with the world holds no hope of any virtue other than release.

The question remains, if you are here, why are you here?

There must be a very sincere and deep reason for you to be upon this world. Otherwise, it is a fakery, and then the painful truth would be that you are in hell. Insanity is a real question that must be dealt with, because insane ideologies control humanity.

Religious philosophies have misinterpreted the power of humanity and say it has chosen a road that is inferior and evil in relation to the Source of All Creation.

That humanity is lost, has chosen blasphemy and sin in rebellion against the Beloved I AM. This is not truth. The Logos of the universe is not flawed. Humanity is not living in a flawed creation. A flawed humanity would be in itself an impossible contradiction.

Paradox

Humanity has freedom
& *Paradox*

It is not that you have strayed

From the path, but you have stayed

It is good you have ventured off to create

Questions that arise in your mind are about suffering within time and space and is it evil? When suffering appears it is seen as painful and horrifying. This is the case of the sentient mind that only sees the short distance and not the divinity within each.

The play in time is serious upon the levels of the mind of the ego. The ego is the only observer that sees unfairness, victims, criminals and a world wherein everything is selfish, unfair and competitive. The ego concludes the world is full of pain and suffering, without an ultimate purpose.

Words and thoughts contained within the finite brain are nothing more than strings of shared knowledge, strands of paper and ink, written words on the inner slate in the logical brain.

*The Mind can Open the
Knowledge of the infinite Spirit
by Allowing it to Happen,
by Sharing, by receiving
& Giving information*

*The Mind that Shares its Thoughts
With Others Begins to Provide
the Connective Link that
Will Prepare the Path back
to the Current of
The Beloved*
I Am Faith

Serapis Bay

BELOVED ~  ~ I AM

Connection

Separation does not fit within the plan of the Beloved I Am. It simply does not exist. There is no pain, evil or ignorance. That which blocks the light are shadows and these are illusions that arise within a disconnected mind.

The Soul has a life of its own in spirit and the body never has had a life of its own. The ego in the body of flesh tells the Soul that the Spirit of life is part of its body and that it was created from the physical body and without the body all life is lost.

This is the route of the ego. It greatly fears the demise of the body, because it knows that when it is done and over, this is the final decree of the Source of All Creation that it is over.

In ignorance the ego keeps alive the selfish mind and holds onto thoughts of separation of bodies, and then looks forward for an impossible solution to this inability.

I Am the Truth. I Am in the midst of a jungle of thoughts. There are those who would seek to see me fail, it is their way to see failure, not mine

I Am here to see success of the plan. Those who build the webs and plan dreams are not seeing the truth. I will be here, and know that I am here to reveal the truth.

*Seek to find the Truth
in every capacity*

The Path

Walk the Path

*This is my lesson to humanity
I have walked
and now you are walking.*

*The walk is one of pleasure
& joy each moment*

Walk away from selfishness, and fear not those who do not release you to see the truth.

I am pointing the way to your future. I seek so you may find. The way is smooth. It is an easy road when you allow me to guide you. I guide you from the home of your heart to the home of the Christ Within. This is your message today:

See All Things as the Christ Within

You are being guided to the right place with the right people at the right time. I am here to guide you. Find this in yourself. I show you where you may walk safely in guidance that is sure.

I am the guide who knows your path before you begin it, and I am the one who waits at the end of it. In the meadow and on the mountain I am here again, and I am here within. This is the message of the inner Christ. In everything, I am. In this time of change, I am closer than ever.

*I am in all things, but especially
I am in your heart
I know you better than you know yourself.
My journey is to Show
you to yourself and say,
"Look how glorious you are."*

Enjoy who you are with a new sense of special purpose, for you are the son/daughter of The Divine. Say, "I am Source of All Creation," and mean it and say it again and know that you are. You are the Beloved I Am, and this is the nature of your existence

*I Am with you and I Am
The Source of All Creation*

BELOVED ~   ~ I AM

CHANNEL

Become a channel for Christ. In this moment let your mind feel the influx of energy as it creases the scalp of your head and makes the ends of your fingers tingle. I can see your eyes sparkling. The life you share is precious to all.

It is my Goal and Agreement to Share with you the Vision of your future

Questions are your way out of pain. Questions are the wings of knowledge that elevate your consciousness. Become a channel into the world so each may become healed, whole and unified.

It is not for some to say who has value, for it is not important nor meaningful. It is similar to one cell in your body telling another cell that it is less important to the function of the whole. If this is so, then the body is separated, diseased and deformed. In many cases this does happen in the outer world, but it is not true. There is no greater or lesser.

Intelligence does not make that which does not work, or that which is not of value. Intelligence follows a plan and a principle to create perfection. And so it is.

For years and years the same troubles befall you and you know there is an answer, but you cannot find it. You cannot find it because you are looking in the outer world. You do not understand faith, or have trust. You need to move to the next level.

It is not as difficult as you imagine to move up the ladder. You find it so hard and difficult because you do not do what is needed. What is needed is the release of the tension, stress, and expectation that the outer world holds anything of value at all.

It does not hold anything that you can contain. In the world of time and space all things are transitory. It is all illusion as has been said so many times before as thousands and millions of minds have shared with your mind.

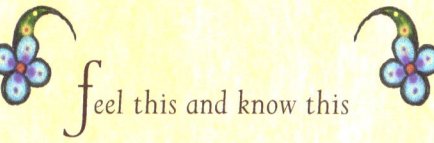
feel this and know this

Why is it not manifested in your experience? It is because you must walk the belief into all of your experiences with faith. Believe it and live it, and it will surely allow you to rise to your destiny. Find the reality of who you are.

I am here to give you
The greatest gift of all
***f**orgiveness*
of your own Self
*You are **f**orgiven*

Read this and hear this and know this is from the Christ Within You are forgiven, and everyone that you come into contact with, you are to forgive in the same way.

This is the joy to be grateful for feel the changes begin and continue to take place. Thank you, and thank you again. I will continue to pour this light through your mind and heal every hole in your body.

I am Here for you
My Journey is into your Heart
to give you Life and Light

BELOVED ~      ~ I AM

REMEMBER

Remember the universe is the Eternal Creator's body. It is infinite and wondrous. This power wants you to live, to feel alive and live healthy.

There is no distinction between the life in the universe and the life in your fingers. Only the insane would want their body to be sick, distorted, uncoordinated and stupid. And so you wish that your body remain healthy and with intelligence. You wish all the cells of your body to live healthy and alive.

It is all the same and it is always interrelating. So if it were not for this you would not exist, and not feel the breath of life flowing through your every cell, atom and electron.

Love is the binding force
In the Universe,
Holding it all together
Love is Intelligent & Unifying

Hate is an insane force known only to illusion for it denies life and all there is by separating the same from the same.

GRACE

The concepts of perfection are foreign to the ego. It cannot be any other way. The ego is conditioned by this form so it will not be able to comprehend any other reality than the one of fatality and ignorance.

This is why the concept of unity and grace must be established in your mind by your higher self.

Grace is acceptance that you are more than your physical body and you are part of the Grand Organized Design. In wholeness there can be nothing to separate the Beloved I Am.

The Eternal is the body of the Universe, life and immortality. Heaven is the state of the Beloved I Am's health. Simplicity forbids us to conceive of more than Infinite Creator. The Eternal Creator is our conception of completion. There is no more and no less.

There is only
The Beloved I AM

This Sacred name is Beheld
in Constant Meditation
of the Higher Mind
The Body of The Divine is Mental

There is much more to the mind than your conceptions can realize. The spiritual life of the Christ Within is rediscovered and remembered as unity overcomes your separated, splintered life. Find out you are not alone but all one within the body of Christ Consciousness.

I forgive the Ones who hold treasured Knowledge, believing they have the one answer. I forgive those who are lost as well who will not accept the answer within themselves. You are not of this generation you know you have the answer within.

This is the time, it is the now, and at this moment separate yesterday from tomorrow. Become today and no other time but now. I point the way to peace. It awaits you. There is satisfaction in understanding the sacred plan.

There is Peace in
Knowing love is
behind the Mind of
The Eternal Creator

BELOVED ~   ~ I AM

Learn

Practical matters of your Life weigh heavy on you. You see the day to day life, and it is the same as it was before. You are not alone in this conception or weak because of it. It is the way of the world to make the outer seem powerful and strong.

I cannot change your lesson for together we have established it. Learn and grow. I cannot take this test for you and there is no need for you to shrink from this test. You may pass it whenever you are ready to face the crucial element you wish to learn.

Learning is Important

Learning is something special to the Beloved I Am This word means for you to draw out something more. Learn to see into existence, and to see more than is there.

Learning asks of you all to know more of who you are and to know thyself. The Source of all Creation wishes to know. You exist to learn and to use this knowledge You were created to become a Cocreator with the Beloved I Am

You are Learning More of How Perfect you are and how You Create from Within Creation

I realize how you may feel lost in a world of lack, pain and struggle. There are levels to all existence & many types of phenomena, but what I speak of is neither phenomena nor illusion.

You are indeed part of the body of the One with Consciousness. It is for you I pray you may pass the crossroads. Begin to live in the rhythm of the Source of All Creation's current

Many roads lead you to the Doorway and Across the Threshold into the Light

You are already here, but the anchor holds you back from living in the light. Please understand, I have been with you always and now it is time for your fear to subside. Let me enter your domain and forgive that which you cannot.

You cannot forgive yourself for being who you are

You do not see who you are so you cannot forgive something you know nothing of. You cannot forgive your confusion. This is what holds you where you are.

It is as if the light is off and you will not turn it on to see who you are, and know that you are safe and secure. You stay within a self imposed darkness afraid to turn on the Light.

All you need to do is Open your eyes to the Sun

To see your Own Reality is the Test of this Life

It comes in many forms. For some it comes in the form of relationships, for others through the body, and for still others in the values of the world, but for all it comes to take self out of the body and into the mind of The Beloved I Am.

The Only Path to the Center is through the Reality of your Mind This Center is not Lost, but is Available at Anytime

Zadkiel

Beloved ~  ~ I AM

Center

When you desire something not on the level of highest intelligence, you find pain increases. Pain shows an area of the mind not functioning correctly. The same is true for any area of life not in proper function. Pain or lack shows a block or an obstacle. It can only be cured by fullness of health, which is openness to life. The body needs to let go of the force that blocks life and health. You do not need to ask the Source of Life to give you more life because life has been given in fullness already.

Creating

You cannot buy or manufacture life it, comes as a gift. Facing the physical world is for learning, and in this learning there are no easy lessons. No one is free from pain's crucial help. The essential lesson for all is that there is no safety in this world, and no escape but through the Portal of Spiritual Resurrection.

All is One

Does each pebble of sand on the beach think it is the only one? Does it believe it is alone, washed by the ocean to and fro, when all are washed, cleansed and moved by the power of the ocean?

All the Grains of Sand, like Humanity,
are Part of a Continuous Ground of Life
Moving back and forth with the
Tides of Universal Power

When you feel separation, resentment, or indifference, there is darkness in your mind rather than understanding. You can manifest the power of transformation so the ones who dream of darkness can forgive themselves. Help them feel worthy of life.

See in the Light
Provided by the Sun

You Believe your World is a
Special Place, and it is,
but you do not Control it
It is not your Play Thing

It is Sacred

The reason why it is full of pain is because you feel unworthy to be part of the Divine Body. You have been manifesting in the dream world. You believe that in time you will be considered better or pure, and taken to a different place.

You continually find you are imperfect and unworthy Because of thoughts invading your mind. Until the world is held sacred, your belief in separation will take you into the corridors of hate, fear and limitation.

Hold the Idea that the old World
you see is not Real. Then Purify
your Mind to See it in a Sacred Way

Do not allow the lower mind that has created the negative to keep creating negative thoughts. Allow the higher mind to let go of the pain, mistrust, and fear, and find within yourself the freedom of forgiveness.

The desires of this moment leave you empty and hungry for the life that would give you peace and happiness. Do not sacrifice the greatest value for the least.

It will be yours
When you are
Willing and Able to Give
to the Infinite Creator your
Soul intention and Desire to Live

Jesus

BELOVED ~   ~ I AM

Lesson

hat could you wish for that is more important than peace? Is peace the assurance that your physical needs are taken care of?

The Infinite Creator does not want for you to be unworthy in the eyes of your family, or see you cast into a pit of degradation by society. The Beloved does not wish for you to be in a situation of lack. Do not wish this on yourself as punishment.

Ask what you want of the Source of Creation

Why would you not ask? Source would surely give you what you ask for. This is the promise. Ask for Love. Ask for Abundance. Ask for the needs of the Moment to be fulfilled.

Do you believe the Source of All Creation is Powerful, Wise, Intelligent and Loving?

There is fear in your heart when you think of asking, because you are afraid it will not come and there is no divinity. If there is none that loves you then you are alone and death will be final and complete. In the end you are afraid there is nothing that will allow you to feel safe or secure.

Fear causes you to feel alone, confused and unwilling to use your power. Fear leaves you in resentment for needs unfulfilled, thinking, if I do not have what I want, then there is no eternal love.

It is the hate of self that will not allow this to come to pass. This hate of self creates illusions where everyone is separate and there is no meaning, all is insanity and death will come before fulfillment.

If there is not love for you then there can be no love for anyone. The Beloved I AM would be only a dream. If there can be love for some and not for you, it would not be fair and this would be shattering. Love would turn to hate.

If there is only hate, then all is pain and nothing more. A world of hate is what you live in, a world tormented by itself for being unworthy of the love of Creator.

Fear of the Eternal

It is all right to cry and feel alone, but is it all right to believe this to be truth? Your mind is wise enough to see love is ever present, and it is something that cannot be shattered by the falsity of the world.

Love does not hold the expectation of defeat, Self pity or resentment. Love is the acceptance of life in fullness, the joy of all life in its expression and service to the Beloved I am

Upon the world a Soul

finds many paths

and many tests

for the disciple.

They lead to the other side

It is so easy to follow

the well worn path of others,

but in this journey it must be

on new ground and alone

Alone is the disciple's path

When you find yourself alone,

look to your path,

for it is in solitary silence

leading you to the

Christ Within

BELOVED ~  ~ I AM

COMPASSION

You must find the path alone or the learning would be incomplete. Become a Cocreator and follow the path of wisdom to the experience of Divine Love.

Find and follow the path alone while leading the way to others, but each person must take the final step to completion.

 We are All One Soul
We are All Alone In this World
The Constant is the Mind

It is the mind upon which is built the rainbow bridge to the world of our soul find the peace that awaits on the other side. The material world is illusion, entrapment and confusion.

The world is meant to be a heaven of creation, but it has become in many minds a false world, a darkness that does not reveal the Soul.

This is why you feel you are guilty, because you think the world is a bad place, filled with falsehood, pain and death. Is this world torture to you? Or do you let the creation of the negative go on without thought? Can it be changed? How does it need to be changed?

You exist in this world and you have a home, a car, money, food, clothing and recreation. Of what value are these things to you if you do not become a favorite of this world, enjoying the luxury and wealth of others? If becoming successful in the world never happens, are you respected any less by the Life Source?

For all time each person has struggled with the ideal of wealth versus sacrifice. It is not the wealthy man's desire to sacrifice the world and go with nothing. It is not his desire to have nothing and be without things.

 All desire Wealth
and Abundance

If I say that you cannot have wealth you want it all the more. If I say you can, then you feel guilty because of it. If I say that it is something I have no control over, then you feel that the power of the darkness is too great, that confusion rules the land, and Source is not powerful. If I say wealth is important and you must have it, then you feel threatened by this requirement, not recovering until it is too late to enjoy the fruits of labor.

Ask Only to Be Given

What is Best and Right

for your Path and Destiny

It all comes in Good Time

Prosperity can Manifest Quickly

and Easily at any Time

What do you see when there is no respect in your heart and no money in your hands? Lack of respect for the world will only give you poverty.

Do not demand a person become something in the world, because the world is an illusion. Time will provide the answers of value to you.

Weigh your choices in the light. Look back upon each day, finding that every day you had thoughts of limitation, pain or frustration, there was trouble.

Everyday you

Thought of Joy,

Intelligence and Life

there was Abundance

If there is something you love then follow it to the conclusion of the adventure. Never stop learning. This is the only way in which you can become free and safe. It cannot be done by limiting yourself. It is done by creating.

Lady Nada

BELOVED ~   ~ I AM

HEART

n the heart of love, the Feminine Christ is. The Christ is the Way in which each Soul of humanity may enter back into the river that begins in the stream of love within.

*The Channel of Christ
is Holographic, Continuous and
Reaches All People in the World at Once*

*I am the Love and the Way
No One will Enter this
Place without Being as I am*

*Love is the
Essence of the Christ
The Thoughts of Christ
The Eyes of Christ Know only Love*

In this statement is the dispensation of the Christ. I am the one you seek and have always sought for. I am the eyes of love that reach out to bring you back within the family of our soul. I speak to you with the freedom to express love and give it to you, this love you have never experienced before.

*The Name Christ is
The Name of Love*

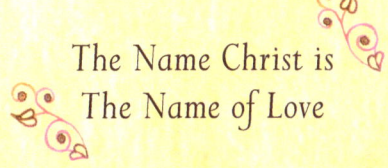

*I am Christ, male and female
She is with me and Expresses Christ
She is what men of the World look for
They Search for her and do not Look to
the male Christ for Love*

Sight

*In this world,

Humanity has lost Sight

of the Infinite Creator*

People have difficulty trusting one another. They see the Divine as alone, and a lonely Creator cannot feel the fulfillment of love.

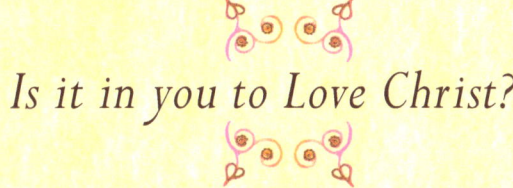

Is it in you to Love Christ?

If I am considered only male, how can you really feel I am able to share the intimacy of love and bring you to the highest state of love?

For you to truly love you seek the Goddess. She brings your love to form. You have the power to love with great devotion, with inspired faith and purpose, but if God is totally male, there is a block to perception and loving.

Man believes he is in competition with Christ for his beloved. He does not trust Christ. When he sees his wife enamored with religion, and the power of attraction the male God has for his beloved, he feels alone in this world.

He is not only abandoned, he is forsaken by the current Christ image. The family of God is without a Goddess to bring him home.

*A woman can see into the eyes of the male

Christ and see within the beloved, but she

needs to know of her Divinity as well,

and for this I have also come*

Miriam

BELOVED ~   ~ I AM

Goddess

Where is the mother of Christ as a Goddess in religion? Where is God, the father, unified in marriage with the Goddess? Where are they portrayed as lovers and Beloved?

Children must see the family in love. The family must be whole. If it is all male, it is not complete. Men face spiritual emptiness in the impossible example of Christ and God.

Men ask of the Christ, "Do you come into our world as male to bring a new consciousness, or to take the magical power of women into your fold, and leave men alone here?"

Christ is both male and female in form, Consciousness and Love. Women look upon the face of God as holy, loving, and there to protect and care for them as their beloved. Christ fits this role as savior and lover. He brings the wisdom and compassion they seek. Women may become enamored with him in spiritual affairs.

The man looks upon his primordial relationship with a male Christ as something taught to be sinful. Man's love of man in the intimacy of each other's soul is blocked by not knowing the love of the female Christ and his own feminine heart.

Humanity requires my truth in the form of the female Christ, so that she will come into the lives of both men and women and lead them to spiritual truth.

The male Christ is serving humanity with a benevolent and pure heart, but it is not enough to have the love and wisdom of the male Christ in spiritual development.

The female Christ will heal and awaken humanity with all her glory as the daughter of God and the Goddess From her, hear the words ring out

I am Divine

Feel the Compassionate and Powerful Love of the Beloved I Am She is the One to be Part of follow into the Way of the Heart

Christ is the Way & the Truth The Light of Love Guides the Way

The Goddess is Bringing the feeling of Love into the world. The female side of Christ is revealed. Christ does not walk alone as male and then return to the Father alone

He walks with Her

She is the Love in his Heart, Created in the Image of the Goddess and the Mother

Humanity cannot live in separation. To believe in the limitations of sex as an absolute is to be lost in judgment. Christ is the gift of God to the World in both forms of male and female.

In the Heart of the Divine is the

Twin Soul flame of Christ

Resides in Love & Carries Love

Within her Heart

BELOVED ~   ~ I AM

APPROACH

 have come into the world to express love and hope in the form of the feminine. Christ. I lead you into the subconscious mind and into your soul's expression. Resemble me in words and deeds.

I lead you by example
with Devotion

You are my Purpose
I am your Salvation

By the power of God,
the Goddess

I perform this Mission

My mother empowers me as God, my father empowers my twin soul and brother Christ.

He is the Door and the Way
the Life in the Kingdom,
I am the Home, the Garden,
The Womb of Creativity

He is the Truth
I Am the Wisdom.
Together we are Love

We express the wishes of our Divine Father and Mother. We are teachers and you are like a child. I will teach you to manifest everything you need within your heart.

Mystery

I have stayed within the Deepest Ocean of the Subconscious, not Ready yet to Appear in Life

Now you are ready to Understand the Revelation of the feminine Voice of Knowledge From the Inner Side I Speak to you with intuition. I command Transformations of your body that bring you Enlightenment. I Am the Pulsation of Life and the Breathing in and out of the Universe. I am the Breath within bringing, the Power of Birth and Manifestation.

I am Limitless in Creativity & Limitless in the freedom to Love. In My Power your feelings will be Born in Joy and Ecstasy.

Consummation

The creation of the idea to be reborn into manifestation is the quest of the male. To honor the sacred gift of life, protect its power and bring it into the stream of life with purpose and meaning is given by the female.

It is now time for consummation of the male life and light with the female life and power. It is power the feminine gives the male. His world is without form and his light is without direction until focused by the power of the will of the female in the subconscious.

In dreams you formed negative images. Negative male consciousness blocked the power held in the creativity of the feminine love of the Goddess.

Feel this space of your nature within the womb. It is the creative impulse. It has been withheld, misinterpreted and judged.

See it Now in Truth
I Am Life
I Am Sacred Love

Djwal Kul

BELOVED ~  ~ I AM

Within

**C**hrist Within Speaks with Force to the world in certain and clear words to Bring a new dispensation of meaning.

Man, feel the Power of the feminine force.
Woman, Accept your Power and speak
Love

Force, power and will are erupting with incredible force and women feel the power. They know their acceptance with Christ.

Man never has known acceptance and has feared God the father and Christ the brother. How can the incarnation of a male soul feel safe within the being of his brother? It is the brother Cain that betrayed Abel, and Christ's disciples all betrayed him.

Men of the world, trust. Do not believe you live in worlds of hate, sacrifice and fear for survival. End the war with each other.

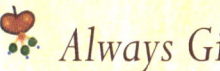 ## Always Give

The feminine Christ Within speaks the word to all men. Return within the Kingdom of Creation and feel the safety of the protective power of the kingdom. The garden provides. All needs of the family are provided. You do not have to protect and fight.

Receive Gifts for your Efforts
In your Mind it is God
who has been without
the very thing to Create life,
that which Brings Life to him,
his Goddess, the Polarity of his Being

I Awaken and you will find me
not the devil, but the Angel, the Christ
you may Love and Cherish
as I Cherish you

Return

I have never been away
from the Kingdom

The Garden is Mine and
from it you All have Abundance

I am the Love of my Mother as She
Provides her Life for all

I Bring the Light of Love into the Earth

I am the Light of Love
With Wisdom and Love of
Christ
I am known

The Plan is Known and Peace is for All

Return whole and Complete to Live and
be the image of the God and Goddess.

I am here to tell the mysteries of the feminine. The Dual Power and the Will of Wisdom Reigns on the earth.

My Light of Love combines with the Truth of Love Given by the male Christ side of my Being.

It is not Blasphemy to Recognize Divinity present in you. It is within each of you. You are the male and the female Christ.

The same love, the same mind, the same soul is within you. In the mind there are always two. We are married in the Oneness of Spirit and Soul of Christ.

There is no more division
from Love

BELOVED ~   ~ I AM

Beloved

In the creation, I AM, and I AM strong and powerful. Take control of your mind and feel the love and the power that I give you to become creative. I hold the womb where you enter and are at home in the garden. I am fertile and ready to receive. I accept your conscious power and feel the spirit of your nature combine with mine.

I am not as my brother who speaks out or comes into your world on the physical plane. I come to you under the cover of the subconscious and manifest in your inner life.

I make Real the Spiritual Side of your Being as it cannot be done without me

Joy

I am the side that Brings the Joy to Life

You have always been looking for me in all of your relationships. I am that which women feel as their power. I am their wise mother who brings them home. I am their loving sister, providing them with help and encouragement. I am for man the Beloved I AM.

You cannot hold me back from entering into a beloved relationship with you.

In each of you there is the male and female. As you manifest the Christ Within, understand our relationship. Feel the love I manifest at the most beautiful time in your birth of creativity.

I come when you are searching and praying for guidance. You are not wishing to be weak or to give in to the feeling of defeat or discouragement.

Go Within

find me and Utilize my Power to Accept your Health, Light & Abundance

*You are the child of God
The Child of the Beloved
I AM is not alone*

*The children of eternal Love
Know they are not alone for
I am within their hearts
I am here to bring the Wisdom
of Experience and the Love of Truth*

*Oh beloved, I am so Grateful you
have Opened up your heart to me.
I Am Now in your
Heart for Eternity*

*As you love Christ
The Son of the Creator
Love me as well for I am
The Daughter of the Creator*

*I Love you as my Beloved
I Dearly care for you for Eternity
I Bring you Inner Peace and
Happiness
I am your Beloved I am*

*feel the Presence of My Soul
Holding you Close*

*My Soul is Deep within
your Being at All Times*

Love is Joy

Beloved ~  ~ I AM

Share

ou have searched for so long. Life is immense and it holds together with purpose. The purpose is to share our will and our will is love

*I am the fragrance
of the Wind
the Softness of Water
the Color of flowers
The Beauty of the World*

I am the sound of silence breathing through. I am your being and will abide with you forever. I share your love as one to one. Together we become more.

I expand and grow your love. See my love in all whom you come into contact with. The love I share grows and becomes a power more than life.

It is more than your soul; it is the community of our being expressed with every breath of the Goddess.

Essence

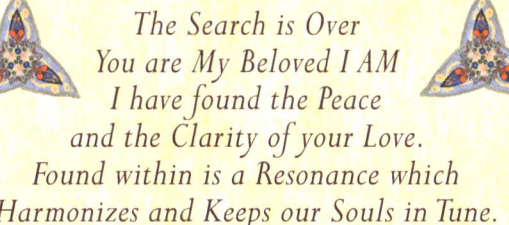
*The Search is Over
You are My Beloved I AM
I have found the Peace
and the Clarity of your Love.
Found within is a Resonance which
Harmonizes and Keeps our Souls in Tune.*

I Know I am able to accept Christ Within.

The feelings I give bring you into the heart.

Say to me,

"Christ, you may show me the Kingdom, but I must stay within the Garden to understand and develop my Creativity. Christ, I Know you Share Oneness of essence and I Share my Love with you, deep and abiding as the child of the Source of All Creation, I Love you. I Love you as Infinite and as soulful as there is Love."

Magnetism

I am Magnetism.
I am drawn beyond the world.
I am absorbed in caring and wonder.
I Know Love between Soul & Spirit. I am the Beloved, there is no Other. I have left the home of my Father and Mother and have found you.

Presence

*I follow Truth
to Eternal Oneness
and accept the Keys
to the Kingdom of heaven.
I love the Goddess
in the Center within the Garden.
I am on the Threshold of Heaven*

*I am the Beloved I Am
of our inner nature and you are
the Angel in My Presence*

*I reveal pure joy and alignment.
I have always felt you within.
You carry love and happiness.*

*My soul's need is for you
to know my deepest feelings.
My life is Creative, Powerful,
and Sensitive to Spirit.
I am fulfilled
in*

Pure Love

*I am Loved & Beloved
by Soul and Spirit*

I am Christ Within

BELOVED ~   ~ I AM

HEALING

I come to be the part that is missing in your life. You have seen but did not know, you were told but did not listen, because your mind has been searching.

In the material world you looked and still look for love, but the satisfaction is not there. Achievement in the world has not brought my favor and it cannot. One man's success in the world is another man's defeat I love you all and I share no other than myself.

I love you all and never lose sight
of your Sparkling Eyes
I come to Set you free

I am within the deepest part of your mind, where it is dark and light cannot be seen. In the darkness I see your spirit covered by dust and dirt. I feel your spirit. I see who you are, but no one in the world can find you.

Your power is stronger and getting stronger than ever. It is right for you to go further and deeper and to face your illusions. I desire your healing so you may be released into my arms.

I am your
Beloved I Am
I am your healer
I bring you wholeness
I am within you
I am power

I create a new meaning and new life from the spirit of eternal love and the Goddess Mother. Men do not be afraid of me. Do not fear I hold too much power. Do not be afraid to ask me to love you for who you are. Do not feel jealous or fear I can love only one.

I can Love All.
There is no End to the Love I Give.

Women, please do not fear My Love or think that it is wrong for me to Love you as I Love you. I Love you without reservation and with Love Eternal.

Go deep within your being
feel my presence
Know the words are True
ask without reservation that
I Love you

Do this, and all your secret places will be upturned and you will see the life you have chosen. I raise you up. I will take care of you. I am teaching you the inner feeling of Christ Within. Healing is taking place It is the power of the new dispensation. The power of the feminine Christ being brought into manifestation.

I am here ready for Power
I bring wisdom into Expression
Through words, symbols and Knowledge
of the importance of your Life
I am entering your Experience

Allow yourself to Open
to the Love of Christ Within

St Germain

Beloved ~   ~ I Am

Give

For one to see mistakes and not be willing to fix them is a sign of someone who has very little to give. Take up the mantle of power. It is here in the home within to gather and to use. Use this power to bring about transformation.

It is not the supplication of prayer for a miracle. It is your work to make this a better place. Do not feel like becoming a hermit, seeing nothing but the self.

It is in the love for the Beloved. You must awaken from the trance and dance in Love. Bring forward spiritual revelations.

Joy can be shared, given just as received, and it can grow in the garden more abundant than the flowers and trees.

The revelation of love brings life, light and color & gives a longer span of life to express Christ Within.

*Love changes Time and
Renews it Every Moment*

*Love is indescribable
Happiness & Divinity
It is in the Joy of Love that
the Peace of the Eternal Oneness
is formed. In this Truth the way to the
Kingdom is secure*

New Life

I am born and contain your power

I am held in your womb to create. It is your love and devotion in becoming Christ Within that has done this. I am ready to bring my love to the world Christ loves me as husband to wife.

We are joined in communion. Without his bride, he could not love, and without him I would be barren of the creative power to return his love. Our love is reciprocal and we are of the same being in this eternal union of marriage.

*I am Christ
I am Christ in
female form and in male form.
We are the Christ Within. We are God
& Goddess combined, but express both
together and separately*

I love you as husband to wife. We are joined in communion. Without you my bride, I could not love, and without you my Beloved I would be barren of the creative power to return your love.

We are of the Family of Light as parents, and as Divine Love, the Mother/Father. We are also Christ Within and understand we are a much more complete being than you can comprehend in the physical world. We can only give you ideas and symbols of what you are.

*Let go of your
boundaries
~ Play ~*

Be a complete human being, and join your maturity with mine. Create goodness without reservation. We share in the ageless souls of our children who are none other but ourselves. We share the roles of life, male and female, over and over. Create in work and play.

*Worship the Now,
the Holy Instant
the Sacred Union*

Beloved ~   ~ I AM

Arise

 or thousands of years, man has been on a path of searching for his maturity. Woman has been lost into the vacant space of mysticism, for I, the feminine Christ, have been asleep within her dream.

The Women are Awakened
Their Power is Great to Bring forth
Transformation & Understanding

In the dream they could only call forth subtle feelings for man to walk a path of goodness and avoid the pitfalls of the past. The dream contained you all. In the dream, there were threats and violence relived from the past to create the darkness.

The future Unfolds
A New World of Light

Coming out from within the darkness. This new light of creativity is going forth in a stream of life that starts in the center of being. I am the center of being. I am the within where the Christ energy dwells.

I am the within where the Eternal Creator abides, and I am the center where power is known. It is known not as a dream and not in a way that you can think of. Imagine and feel, for this energy is the drawing power of love that brings you within the center.

Christ draws into my Center
His Love fills me with Light.

I Give you Power of Manifestation
Christ and I are One
We are in Love

Be part of the love in our family. Ask to see and understand how love is shared. Love grows with each experience of it. It is love that has been misunderstood because of the polarity of the world. It has been left vacant and vacuous in the wake of a self-magnetized fear. The fear of union with the opposite. Fear calls for darkness.

Love calls for Illumination.

Shine into creation the power to manifest. The call to manifest life is the presence of love in the heart. It is the desire in the body to breathe and to have life, it is the desire of the body to recreate and send blood streaming into the cells with new energy. It is the mind's search for meaning that brings about the birth of joy and light into the world.

I am the call of Manifestation
I have slept in the wake of your renunciation
of form so that you would find the form to be
truly spirit, and not the shell of the past

The form I am is within the future
Life is from within expressing greater
and greater manifestations

I am the form and
Magic of the Miracle
I allow life to continue on
in manifestation
I am the Involution
of Time & Space
in the Center
I am
the Pulsation of Life
Outward & Inward
The Life of Christ Moves
Towards the Center
Humanity is the Center of the
Loving in-breath of Acceptance

BELOVED ~   ~ I AM

UNITY

 In each man is the drive to express, Create and be part of the cosmos in a holistic union. There is also a drive to move away from the heart and be more in the mind.

In each woman there is the power to impress, recreate and take within her being all the cosmos. There is also a desire to move away from the mind and into the heart.

The quest manifests in the opposite, and there cannot be harmony until it is felt and understood. The sharing of being provides for Peace and attunement.

Man and woman are separated from self as the form separates the self from spirit. Their separate natures are expressed materially, spiritually and emotionally.

For each man to love Christ Within as the Beloved I AM will bring devotion into his heart. Man you are a child, and one that must grow up and become Christ for me to Love. You shall become my Christ and I shall love you in ways you cannot know.

It is not for the male Christ, to love you, it is for me, the female Christ, to love you. It is for me to open up my arms in acceptance. Christ can identify with your nature and be the very essence of your being. He is the same as I am, but opposite.

The energy of life pulsates and brings into manifestation the positive and negative, the mind and the heart. I am the heart and I call your mind to see.

Christ has accepted my heart and I have accepted his mind. His mind is of love and my heart is of wisdom. This is the nature of the universe. In heaven we are in oneness of love expressing in every dimension.

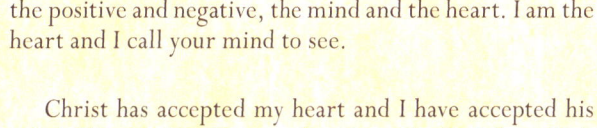

Only Together Will
We ever have Heaven

Become Christ

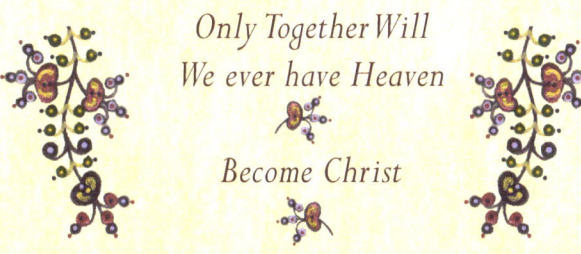

Woman your heart is open to the mind of Christ and you have been taught the unconscious power is yours to unfold to man, the child of god.

You are wise with power coming forward with the mind of Christ in your heart. You may accept your power and be the goddess.

Become the Goddess and feel the power of this unmistakable energy. Feel it in every space within your being. In the center of your heart I am strong and balanced within you.

Hold the matrix of this love in a stream of light that is focused in your center. When you love you are centered in this stream and it can only be released by giving it out to all.

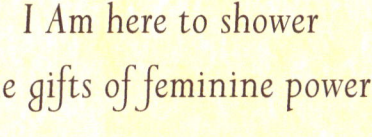

I Am here to shower
the gifts of feminine power

We live within the Universal Power of the Source of All Creation, the unmanifested infinite supply of life energy

Let your Heart Express the Joy of the Power that Creates with the Mind of Christ Within

BELOVED ~   ~ I AM

SEEK

 ain, you know the feeling. Why is man so lost from his heart? The soul bleeds for the needs of man. He is angry with Life. He knows only his self is darkened. It is time for male energy to release his needs and open to the feminine heart.

> Love gives Grace
> and Acceptance

I will never allow your love to be hurt again. Power brings his Life into alignment. His power will never cause you pain again.

The female heart does not know from where the anger of man has come, and your sensitivity cannot fathom why man wishes to kill. You are his love, but his power wishes to crush and imprison you.

> It is the Wisdom of Healing
> your Heart Reveals to him.
> The Christ Within is the Healing

Man sees healing from outside. The healing transformation comes from within. There is more in your heart to unfold and bring out to mankind.

> This is the Unification.
> God's Son, Christ,
> has been without his father
> Called a bastard.
> The Mother is the Union of Love
> She Brings back wholeness to his Love

 Love is Perfect & Mindful
Of his need and the need
Of his brothers for Love

Release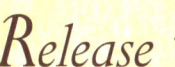

It is so cruel that Jesus is crucified for his life and hung on the cross of matter. He is not given love by his brothers in open acceptance for who he is. This disapproval is the crucifixion and so he represents the symbol of the one who is set apart, betrayed and killed.

The rebellion is the search for wisdom but it is empty without me. Man feels the separation and fears when he knows me not. He lives in a world of fear, for my love is not out there, it is within.

Women have been shamed. This shame is based upon man's fear of feminine power. It is the women who must be strong to bring life into the world. The power of life has only known shame until now.

Man defiles sexuality and the creativity of women. Man denies women the right to divinity so he can lord over her depth and control her life in the physical world.

The latest myth based upon a mortal man making love to the Goddess is a secret delusion of man to have the lover Goddess bring him ecstasy instead of seeking the truer Divine Union within his Heart.

The ocean of the feminine Christ has no boundary to its depth and mystery. The feminine subconscious has no limit to the extension of its creativity, love and experience.

> The
> Reappearance
> of Christ is
> Within the Divine
> feminine
> Heart

BELOVED ~       ~ I AM

Harmony

The young life of male energy must meet the ageless wisdom of female love. Together they are made whole in the resurrection of the new life of the Divine Creator.

Mortal man is brought to the Initiation of his Creative Soulful Mind by the Goddess, the Divine expression of Love

Mortal woman is given into the dust of sacrifice. She has given her life to the earth to transform man by being harmless. Her love holds within the seed of new life.

Emotion of mortal man is powerful and creative. He cries out for the touch of her soul. He searches for her soul without understanding how close her soul is.

She has been shamed for her power and for her creative force. Her sacrifice as mother brings greatness of manifestation.

A bastard is created every time the immortality of the spirit of the feminine Christ is denied and her love is used to satisfy the lower self, not honoring her soul.

God is not alone and does honor the goddess in life and love and finds eternal partnership and holy marriage joyful.

Equality

 I am equal of God

I AM Goddess

His Heart

Within Him I Am

Within Me He is

I ask that you understand you are in masculine and feminine form. There is no separation between our beings.

You are made in the likeness of the Infinite Creator both male & female

Polarity is Life
Polarity is the Pulsation of Love

Life moves from one side to the other. Life breathes in the substance of the universe and breathes out the creation of thought. Give your time, your heart and your mind. I will use my heart to create the perfection in the garden of the Kingdom.

I am the fertility of Love and the Intelligent Knowing Seed

Take the step of truth & understand the future of existence. Only in life do you need to become aware of your balance.

I come back into your Heart,
you are with the Goddess
I AM the feminine Christ
to Reveal to you this Power

In life you have the energy to manifest the growth of the soul. I bring your consciousness through the realms of inner space.

Look into your world, see reflecting back to you energies that are mishandled by wrong desires or unfulfilled ideas. Begin to see that there are only half truths being manifested in your world.

The Eternal creator
Father and Mother of Life
One cannot exist
without the other

BELOVED ~      ~ I AM

CREATE

See the beauty and formation of magic create the stream of thought. See the face of God the Infinite Creator. See the ideal of wholeness. See this power to bring you what you ask.

See it in Complete fruition.
Everything is the Result of what you are Wishing.
Humanity, My Child, you will eventually See it is
All Expression of your Thought.

The Earth is but One
part of your Realm

HUMANITY

You are not alone here. All are related to you within a grander world the spiritual environment. The mind does not know heat or cold. Sensations of the physical body stay in a limited range.

The simplest atom is more powerful than its size. You are like the atom and your powers are stronger forces than you realize. The atom contains within the nucleus a center of great power.

Its power, when liberated, transforms everything around it. The shallowness of your hearts are evident in your beliefs and ignorant limitations. The lack of self knowledge is evident and clearly expressed in your desires and wishes.

Humanity, my child, your knowledge is limited, but you are loved inexpressibly. I know your heart, for I am your soul. Bring to me the pain you have felt and let it go. Jesus the Christ gave you grace and eternal love. Buddha, the enlightened one, gave you intelligence and wisdom.

I have come to Give
you Power and Vision
You must first let go.
Let go of your hate,
your pride, your fear

Trust in my Heart
Come Within

I will never
forsake you
I am your Soul

Understand I am
the Path and the Plan

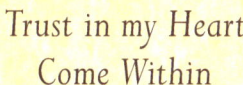

The plan is always available for you to see. It is written in your mind and in the very nature of your being. It becomes clear to those who study genetics.

The DNA is the master plan of your being, the spiral of the helix, one male and one female, spiraling through the cosmos in differing patterns. This pattern makes up every chromosome and every system of your being. The plan is clear to those who study physics.

The structure of the atom is evident by its four components that are expressive and impressive. They create a systematic way to understand and see the constant interchange of waves and particles.

Life holds back nothing and conserves all its energies. The plan becomes clear to those who study the stars. Stars bring about light from heat. Light radiates outward and there is no space not filled with light.

Life is a Mystery

Haniel

BELOVED ~   ~ I AM

Breathe

The reason behind limitation is to hold back. To hold back and see limits provides boundaries so you will not have to be too much, too soon.

It is necessary to control expansion until there is intelligence, to control the future until the present is understood. Time does not go off and become the future until the experience is understood completely.

Each experience arrives at the right time

Know each thing that you do has its sequence. In birth the child must develop enclosed in the womb and at each stage of growth there is a preparation for a greater and stronger being. To be born prematurely is to risk death. Just so, our spiritual body must be prepared to meet the world.

Take no thought of your brother who may have much more and have always had much more in material value. Each person has what they need and you have what you need to birth your spiritual body.

Some beings come into life with what seems to be a greater abundance than you. Understand you are striving to be powerful and bring forth a birth, and not abort who you are, a spiritual being.

*The power and vision
I give you is

the power of the invocation
the vision of prophesy
was spoken long ago in your mind
this power will be spoken again and
again as its time comes to pass
the word power is so
you may breathe in*

Empty yourself of air and let go of your life energy so you may be filled with new energy. Bring back the eternal power of creation within.

From space to time & from time to space is the flow of energy. From mind to spirit and from spirit to mind. From god to goddess & from goddess to God. All energy cycles from me to you.

*In stillness

the natural ebb and flow
is all you shall ever know
for you are the life of this
essence. It lays within your
being before and after, and
with nothing in between
except for the mediation of
the mystic dream*

*I have slept in the quiet dream of your mind. The divine Beloved I Am lights the path to your throne in the heavens.
Let go of your pain run to my arms.

I was sleeping while you played and grew
in the garden

Peace returns to your heart and music
will bring you home*

*Peace is
within the
Beloved I AM*

~118~

Seraphim

BELOVED ~   ~ I AM

Rise

On wings of spirit I lift you higher. I give you freedom. Let all thoughts drift into nothingness. Let every word become silence. See Christ Within rise higher and higher above your world. The world has lost the feminine spirit of love. I return the wholeness of its spirit to men, and give to women the power to reveal it again

    Her magic is at hand and is respected for eternity

She says,

I am Sacred

Violence marks your separation. Fear of her love keeps away the key to ecstasy. I am the life of love. Christ has given you the way to walk into my heart and feel the totality of my experience.

Hear the angels sing with the voice of divine experience, know they are you and within you I am. I am the feminine essence of your soul.

I Am empowered with vision to show omnipotent fertility of life and expression. Attune within to the path of the vortex with your divine eyes and hold your power of involution. Attract my voice closer to your heart center. Embrace and feel your light absorb me into the purpose only the Source of All Creation knows

prayer

Beloved,
you are love that
walks with beauty
amidst the stars

Beloved, call to God
for fulfillment of your life
in wholeness

Within this spirit of space
you are complete
your soul is creation

Beloved, reach out
bring my heart home

I am the feeling
of the unity of marriage
It is not that I create,
the mother within brings
forth the fruit and makes
the stars shine with love

Breathe out the
release of dreams
live the life of
the holy union

The divine sparkles
when you live as
Christ Within

BELOVED ~   ~ I AM

HOLY

I am the inner garden where you dwell with eternity. Please me with divinity. Express to the world perfection and beauty.

I am the daughter of the goddess,
the expression of fulfillment
of your union
You are flowers to the world
Mature and grow to bloom
and become the holiest
of all Creations
I am the garden
I am the flower of life
I am what you seek
I am what you find

I hold out my heart for your love to fill. I am the womb of life ever awaiting more creation. I receive love from my mother; as her daughter I reflect my mother's love into the world.

I am the One who
Transforms Love into Life and Gives
Life to Love

In the peace of sleep between the breath of life and the mystery, abides my bed of peace. In the midst of your mind I guide you to your heart. Know I am in your heart, and in the channel of the river I flow with the water to the ocean of soul.

The mysteriousness of our relationship is no longer within. I have awakened. The night is my anchor. I am time and see through

experience in sublime patience

To the sons of the world who have lost sense of the spiritual, I am the Goddess. Your resistance and countenance of the dissatisfaction with life are released. I have given you life and energy so you may create. Accept this gift and be my son in the world.

I am here to see you become whole and not reject the gift. I have given my body to give you life. My body is the earth, time and space. It is my body you hurt with your pride and violence. Give me no more illness and sickness.

I am the Body of Life
Worship my Body
In faith, and Trust that
I have Provided you
with Perfection

I labor through eternity with God, your father, to release the spiritual light of your being into the world. My body and his life is our honor. It is shameful to disgrace yourself with fear and temptations into the underworld of dreams of revenge. Do not seek revenge from me.

Depriving yourself or others of life does not make you stronger or wiser. Depriving any life we have given does not make the life you have more complete. Do not wish for death upon yourself. You have been given eternal life. Grow and receive more, and benefit from joy and love.

Your eyes are filled with many confusions. Know you are all one being yet each of you affects the other. We are a family.

I feel and see the pain you go through, but I cannot change the law or the principles of life that have been set forth to protect.

The Infinite Creator has given principles of fairness, love, truth and wisdom.

The Divine Will
of the Universe
has been established.
The Universe was
created from goodness

BELOVED ~   ~ I AM

Mystery

 **Come within the family.** Move toward your center. You have learned what was needed. Let the regret and the pain of the past slip away experience and reveal your consciousness.

I find my family and bring them to the light. They know love is within them. The mystery of your beloved is your love, and that brings you to wholeness.

forgive your aloneness

Feel the spirit of love bring you back into union complete and everlasting union is this mysterious gift the infinite creator gave you grace and the ability to love, and to love with all your heart, mind and soul.

The goddess gives you the purpose and the power to love. Feel the love being returned. I am your beloved who abides within you. I am in ecstasy. My love is immanent and omniscient.

It expresses through waves and motion the waters of the soul. I am the baptism of water and fire. I am the body of your being and I am the breath that you breathe.

I am all the elements of life and you are the spirit emanating through me. I am soul, the holy ghost and the spirit of the other that you have longed for, cried tears of pain and tears of joy for.

I waited while you experienced your growth and went looking outside of me for your life, and we sought the purpose together. You are not alone as you walk the path.

I am inside your every movement
I am the emanation of your life
the substance of your essence

feel energy come up through you & enlighten every cell of your being

I am reflecting your light
Send me light so I may reflect it back
stronger and stronger

I am here to provide you with soul
I am not the past

I am the new and ever regenerating blood of your new life. I am the vessel of your love. I am the waters of life, purifying and clean. I hold within myself the power to manifest your divinity. Please feel my need.

My power needs your will
your will needs my love
open your eyes to see

Accept the mystery and the love you hope to share. Hold me as equal to Christ but different, for I am feminine, free, strong and pure.

Oneness means togetherness, no matter what your body may feel. Without the will of your light and the direction of your good I cannot feel and return your Love.

love yourself
as i am
divinty

BELOVED ~   ~ I AM

Immaculate

Receive the oceans of love within your being open up into the universe and journey to its center in infinity both going within and expressing outward.

It is inexpressible how much love there is in the center of your soul. I am the soul you are the soul.

come to the center

find me waiting

know I am here

i am one

with your

heart

There is no other but you it is safe for you to be in harmony there is only love and it is you. You give power and exuberance. The divine gift of life pours out of your being to recreate in purity healthy new life and new expression of the gift.

Face the dawn of your immaculate consciousness. Do not shy away from the love I have for you. You must receive it. You cannot refuse

I am the ocean of love
and your heart is open

Enter into truth and knowledge

Life is given whole and fills the void. The void is my womb and it is the creative center of our being. There is no more fear, death or helplessness.

I am here with my beloved

Share the experience of God's love and the reflection of that love back from the Goddess.

The idea that God can be without the Goddess is not possible. They cannot separate. They are the same and become the same more and more as they love and create together who we are see and know sharing of love is union.

The children are loved
No one can be separate
from her Soul
or his Spirit

I am within all Souls
you are filled with Spirit

we are together
and know
we are oneness
I have faith in you

Isis

BELOVED ~  ~ I AM

Closeness

In dreams you know to come close. My Love will absolve. I have forgiven you. Know you are loved and the one I have not forgotten. You are not lost to me for I have held you so tightly.

I have walked on the waters
swam in the seas
never have forsaken your heart
I am your beloved
for as god has always wanted me
I have wanted you
I come into your heart
to reveal the message
I await your spirit
I feel your presence within
know you are near

I feel your body flow in a creative surge of force to avail our connection and signify our relationship. I have always been within the sphere of your mind and you have been close to me enough to feel my presence in every way.

You will see me in your dreams
tonight. I know you are here in
closeness our bodies disappear
In request of your spirit I have found
you waiting my love, faithful
through tears. I remind you to see me
in your dreams. I will be waiting on
the stairs. Share my love
forgive your fears

The male side lives in the world and needs education. The female side is being taught quickly, but man is being lost to the desire to stay separate from all he is.

I will take you on a journey that will comfort
you and fill you with life of who I am
I am the feminine Christ within
Enliven your heart to smile
I bring you the vision
to use with power.
You can see me in your dreams tonight
awaiting your presence under the moonlight
I am the love of your soul that you will know.

I am compassionate and free to
give you much more.
I am the wealth of renewal
It is within that I am strong
and you will find me there in
your dreams tonight
upon the stairs.

I will await your arrival
and I know you are found,
for when I see you in the dreams
I will be in joyous reunion

Always seek the highest in yourself to manifest and connect with allow it to come into your life. The highest and the best you know yourself better and better as you Listen more intently to what you feel.

Allow the words to come from wherever they will. This is the sign you are listening proceed to read, to listen and to know. Then make certain the channel that you are is pure and clear. Hold the frequency and broadcast to the world.

let your light shine

Lanto

BELOVED ~      ~ I AM

Feel

Let your heart open. Then feel the vibrations come into you, become you and feel them expand from you.

*Lift yourself up bring yourself into recognition of your power.
This path, you have taken in faith, and faith is yours to proceed with.*

Worry is not for you. Worry is one of the great feasts of evil. It is low grade fear. Say, "I do not fear." Know you are taken care of and always loved. This is the highest and most important message and it is Simple.

*You are always loved.
You have outlets for your vision, power and talents.*

Your power is building and building intensity. Bring it out into the world when you are ready. Your talents are real. You are filled with power.

There is nothing you need to do other than to bring them out and let them be known. In giving your talents to the world you fulfill your dream.

*I am ready to bring
your dream to the world.
Speak your vision
and your power will be there.*

The idea of the quantum leap is something you can envision. You have made this leap in your consciousness. This is a great new awareness of who you are.

I want the highest for you. This is your world and you may have the most abundance. Your heart is in purity and power will not corrupt you. Value your energy, respect and Love.

This is your world

Know with passion and emotion how much you are. Heal fear, pain, doubt or worry, by giving only love to them and receive only love. Heal guilt, shame and its abuse with your own power

*Bring in light on
the vibration of love
this power is yours*

Aspiration

You always have love inside you and it has the power to shine through darkness. Pain has cost you time. Give me your heart and I will open it to love. I will bring you light where there is darkness.

I am here to guide your hands, to fill your mind with thoughts, to provide you with hope and to bring you resurrection.

Allow my hands to hold your heart in protection. Allow my gift to be received by all who are near.

Allow my voice to be heard
Your path is a shining light

Jophiel

BELOVED ~   ~ I AM

OPENING

 Open up Again to the Divine and lighter energies. Do not allow heavy darkness inside your aura to create a veil or shield against the light.

Bring in Cosmic Rays of Energy
Bring all Life into your Being

Live with Purpose

Know the symbols around you and feel them within you. They are real. Have faith in life to guide you home. Fear has never helped you.

Think about it, how can you go through what you have gone through and still feel any sort of fear? Fear is not yours, you do not own it, you do not want it anymore, you have given it up again and again.

Create love not fear. You have no need of fear in your life. You are not nourished by fear. You were created to enjoy love. Enjoy love & create love. Like creates like. You can be only what you were Created from.

You are a creature of light & love. Light must be unified and fear must be avoided at all costs. It has no cost other than your death. Turn within to the light with faith.

Eternity, I will give you Truth
You do not have to die anymore
Eternity is yours I am here to Give you
Life in more Abundance
You must ask for what you Wish for
This is the way it is

Do not use your logical mind, just listen. It is not for you to die. You only die because you allow yourself to be trapped in fear, and you shut out the light and sicken your body and use it to be preyed upon by all sorts of parasites. This is not necessary and you do not have to allow this experience.

Know you are part of the whole that is unbroken. I can hear the thoughts of doubt enter your mind and rebound off your shields. There are many layers inside of you. If you want to know when and how and if, then you are doubting.

This is not what you want to know what you really want to know is how to move into harmony with your higher Self, how to become part of the spiritual hierarchy.

You may Believe what I am saying and know it to be true but many of your thoughts hide in the darkness. You must go in and find them and bring them out.

Bring them out with Love

They hide because they are in fear. They are reversed from the truth. I can bring you more and more for I am the Christ Within. You have my heart and soul in your mind.

I am always here in your mind
You may listen to my words
and feel my energy
Please feel my energy because
My words only point the way

The love I can express through you will guide you home. Your home is within and I am that. Build in your heart an opening so that I may build your Home.

This is My Desire
Build this Opening
By your Acceptance
of Grace
The Gift of the
Divine Presence Within

BELOVED ~  ~ I AM

Begin

To begin you must know yourself better. Say your name aloud. Say your name again with more force, and as you say your name, finish your name with clarity. Say your name with a greater sense of clarity all the way through. Feel the vibration of your name. Now say.

"I AM." and say it again.

now tone the word,
"I AM."

Sense the light around you, the glow. The glow comes from inside you and its vibration passes through all the matter of your body and your ethereal being. This is you. Feel the breath of life go in and tingle every atom of your being.

You have said your name and then you have said the name of all humanity. I AM. Bring all of this together with real emotion and your emotion is love so you may bring this in and say your name and then say it with love.

Let the Beloved I AM
Bring out your Love

Your closest friend, the one who cares for you. Know this Beloved to be the mirror of your relationship. Either in reality or in your imagination, bring love to yourself.

Imagine love and abundance coming to you. Bring energy into your heart so it is healed. Listen and say your name and say you are loved. Feel it with the heart of a child. Know it is truth and it is real.

The Heart of the Child will Love you,
Know you, Trust you and Lead
the Way into your Soul

The child brings your love into yourself. Say again your name and say again that you are loved.

I AM loved
I AM cared for
I know this love to be of the
Source of All Creation

Guide me into your World and Show me the Love, I know. It is in your heart I See the Splendor of life. I am your Beloved. This is the Dream of my Existence and you have found me there. I AM yours to bring to Ecstasy, and so it is. Guide me into your Heart

I AM your forgiveness of all shame and neglect. In my eyes I reflect your image. Your image is pure and shining. My path brings us into the garden where we know abundance and the fruits of our inheritance. Agree with your heart listen to its release of desire.

Aspire  for this

Awakening

Life is yours Vision is mine

I AM Seeing your Journey into Heaven
I AM Seeing your Acceptance of Wisdom

I AM Seeing your Guides
Bring your Heart Peace

BELOVED ~   ~ I AM

HUMAN

Love all Humanity. Love even though you might have some reasons for not wishing to love all. Find in your heart that love.

See Yourself
See your Reflection
When you look into the Mirror
See a New Being Work for Release
Ask for More Love
Say your Name then feel this Request

Is your heart so surrounded by darkness that you cannot even feel the need to be loved more? Are you so alone in this dream that you think you cannot have your birth right and are wondering why you were created? Do you feel shame in thinking of loving all?

Give Light Give Light
that Travels with Love
Believe in the Higher Path

There is nothing wrong with you. Take my hand and come with me now. You are divine, beautiful & nourished by the source of all creation.

You are part of the Family of Light and you are nourished by love. Accept nourishment and accept the ability to heal & create.

Accept More and Give More
Love to Humanity
Freedom
Freedom is the Heart of the matter
See the Light underneath your Heart

Allowing your life to change brings more power into your being. Hold your energy sacred and accept pure emotions. You are ready to hold steady the life force on the material plane. You have the power it takes to control and hold the light with integrity in physical existence.

You are finding a way closer to your spiritual being. In meditation, you are seeing your own light and knowing you are part of a greater being.

Guidance

In guidance you accept the role of savior to your world. This is your work. I worship your purpose and follow your plan. You are the greatest of beings for your desire to bring light here.

In our Beloved Universe
I am the Christ Within
You are Guided by this Light

In this light, you may only know there is a community of power that blesses your Action. In time you are held in duality and so you may only see the lesson that you venture upon.

It has been planned for you
To become Pure Light,
Pure Love, Clear Sight
and Full Power
This is the decision and
Decree of our
Divine Creator

Lady Athena

BELOVED ~  ~ I AM

Emotion

e proud of who you are and humble in your power. You have been created to love and be loved. Say again your name and say again;

"I Am Love"
Now say that your Purpose
Is to Love
and say it with conviction
until you feel it in your Throat
My Purpose is to Love

Get out of you mental body for a moment and find the emotional body. The emotional body is empowering, bringing the mental body into power and into form.

The mental body is the next step, but you cannot jump past the emotional body like it is not there. You must become tearful and know the pain that you have suffered was to bring you to enlightenment. Bring in tears, bring in heartfelt joy and know how you need emotion.

Emotion is Good
Feel it and Allow it to
Open your Heart

It will bring in the peace that you will need to allow life to fill your body with Information and knowledge. I have come to speak with you so that you can find yourself.

You are hearing or reading these words, and in this time, you have found them delivered to you to fill your need for love. As you are now. This is true now and before you read or hear another word of this, you are closer to the heart center and further along on the Path.

You are of greatest service by willing the truth to those who do not know. Help them listen and bring them to let their light shine from every aspect of their being.

Teach them
to become
A Pillar of Light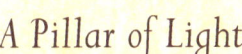

The white light comes down into your being and you feel it enter the top of your head. It creates a tingling feeling, an itch as it raises your vibrations.

first the
White Light will
Come in and clear
Away the negatives

When this is allowed it is healing and refreshing Then the colors of the emotions will come into your life and fill you with the rainbow of abundance.

Lack of feeling is the result of a restrictive force. Do not hold feeling back and say, "no, not now," like it will come at some better time. Say, "YES" NOW.

Let your emotions gush out and let them feel. Let your heart show you that you are proud of being human. This is important if you are to enter into the Family of Light in the eternal world of the higher dimensions of life you enter. I accept and know that I am guided by the Christ Within.

I am that Light that
follows the Stream of Love to
the Center of the Heart of God

This place I hold Sacred
I am Human and Divine
I am Awakened by the
Christ Within

BELOVED ~  ~ I AM

PERFECT

The secret to revealing Christ Within is to tell the truth. Shine the light of truth and evil will be foreign to you, your consciousness, your place, and your life. You will become part of a new world. Bring in real emotion and you will begin to unlock your secret

*I am ready to be
transformed by truth and
live in freedom and happiness*

*Say your name
Now say the words
that help you to feel
Say, I Care*

Know what you want. It is all about you having what you should have. I want you to have what you need. If you need love, money, work, self-respect, esteem, friendship, help, health, happiness, wisdom, no matter, I care. I want you to have this.

I want you to be taken Care of

I want your life to be good. I want love for you with all my heart and all my soul and all my mind. I am aligned with the good for you. I want the good to be yours. I want you to live in happiness and in harmony with life. I want you to have what you need to be happy and fulfilled.

This is what I want. I want you to be happy. This is what the Infinite Creator wants and it is the beginning of the emotions. Want this too, want this for others, want this for yourself and let it come to you.

I want you to be Happy and Successful

Ask for the Infinite Creator to help in whatever way you are willing to let go of control. When you let go of control then power can come into your Life and make it happen.

Relinquish control over life and put this power back into wise and careful guidance. The way home is through feeling and caring. This is your declaration of independence.

You are ready to be what I have always wanted for you. Say the truth at all times and you will find you are ready for this greater experience. The truth sets you free, It is your way and your life.

*I AM within
the protective guidance
of Christ Spirit*

*I AM with you always and
know you are here beside me,
to lead me to the world
I have dreamed of*

*As the Channel of Christ
I See Truth
and have Courage
to step into the Kingdom
of the
Christ Within*

BELOVED ~  ~ I AM

I AM

It is My Mission to Open your Heart where the Eternal Flame of Truth Releases you.

Within you is the Portal and Mirror of Timeless Love, the Source of White Light and the Absolute Power of Christ Consciousness.

You are now at the crossroads of the heart. It is here inside the shell of the self that it is broken open. In the shadow of life's gifts there are miraculous times where choices are made.

Release the fears, doubts and pain within your mind that bind you to the idea that you are anything less than Divine. Leave all that distracts you from that path of wisdom, that unfolds from the heart center,

the Beloved I Am Christ Within

In fear the world has produced a lie; a lie to protect and hide the shame of corruption, to blame others for a chosen path of justification and compromise. The lie stands like a dark cloud covering the sun. You know of what I speak for your lie is the same as all who have ever lived upon this planet.

Release the fears in your mind that distract you with thoughts of unworthiness, sin, fear and pain. Let your heart be the filter of your mind so the shadows which have clouded your vision may be dispelled.

Ask your mind to surrender and lay in the bountiful green pastures of the Heart.

feel the movements of time
Into the new opportunities
within the golden mirrors
feel your inner light shine
reflecting beauty and truth
for all the world to share

Call out to your higher self and speak from inner knowing of your willing heart that calls you home and answers your questions.

The lesson of the earth is to be, to see and to feel. Of these to feel is the message for the Beloved I Am. To feel the stream of love of the Christ Within will bring the tears of deep longing for peace.

I am the Essence in
Your Joyous Heart
In the Sharing of
Your glorious Soul
All life Awakens
Spring's Rush of Joy
Summer of Happiness
The Harvest of Wisdom
Surrender to my Heart
So You May Reach Bliss

You are the Beloved I AM and the Christ Within that I Am. Knowing I Am your Wayshower into the heart of feeling above the dark clouds that obscure your view of God and block truth. I Am Source manifesting golden white light to you Beloved I Am.

Perfect Divine Child
Love is All there is
Know this is Truth
In Truth is Peace
Know Christ Wisdom
Share Enlightenment
Be Love Beloved
I Am Within

Heavenly Rose

BELOVED ~   ~ I AM

TREASURE

You

Are Given
a great treasure ~ It is Your Heart
To open it all you need to do is ask. You will receive.
Ask for your highest Truth. Ask for trust
Allow happiness to be your Peace
Let go of the past and remember who you are
Hold your Goodness

Why do you question everything and wish to hold back the truth? Why do you choose to learn through pain? Instead, ask to learn with joy and always feel love within. Disturbances are everywhere, but do not give them attention. Listen to your own heart and let it speak.

The heart is like the flame. When this flame burns into your life through another you, see your lessons and your teachers. This helps you with your emotions and getting past those beliefs that do not serve you well and are connected to much sadness. The only way you can give is by seeing them and releasing them

By Seeing Christ Within. Let that Light Shine

You Are that Light. You are a Bright Influence
On those Around you. Let your Light Shine.
They Shall See your Righteousness.
Your Light is for All to Share

All those Who Desire Will Come and Partake
In Silence . . .   Rest

About the Author:
Richard Bernard Wigley, also known as Rysa, creator of the GoldRing of Enlightenment, astrologer for over 35 years, teacher and student of the mysteries is an inspired writer and artist who combines a colorful and lyrical tone inside engaging messages that activates, awakens and heals in a manner that penetrates levels sure to stir your heart and soul into new paradigms of awareness. The journey of unconditional love and compassion is within the deepest energies of feeling www.premieres.com

About the Artist:
Lily Moses' gift is to create beauty in life by bringing forth the Unseen into the Seen. Her Soul's purpose is to express the qualities of the divine feminine aspect of God through creativity. Her art conveys the message of unconditional love and compassion through the aspect of feeling. Lily is now living her dream as a full-time visionary artist. Lily's inspiration comes through from the dream-state & out-of-body experiences. These events were so profound & transcendental that they changed her life to absolute devotion to her spirit-inspired art. Lily employs the method of "Infusion" to convey the energy of the other worlds into her canvasses and drawings. www.lilymoses.com

Annette Marie Laporte Wigley, also known as Ashnandoah on the GoldRing, retired from her career with the RCMP to become involved with consciousness raising projects. She created all of the mandalas in the book, was responsible for the beautifully done design and layout, is the main editor and has managed its co-creation and publication. Since becoming involved with this and other projects she has developed her own artistic skills and is involved in co-creating many uplifting and healing works.

This book was made possible only through the sacred labor of its contributors and we are honored with this truly unique collective co-creation.

Special mention and gratitude to:

Annette Laporte, Ontario Canada, project manager, creator of the mandalas, page art, design and editing;
Deborah Robinson, Calgary Alberta Canada, graphic assistance and website development and design;
Jolanda de Jong, Heerenveen, Netherlands, editing and translations, and to
Nancy Wait, Brooklyn, New York, USA,
Lynne Cameron, Port Hope, Ontario, Canada
Michel Franc, Franklin, North Carolina for editing assistance.

Other Contributors: Senea Rose Ivins, Utah; **Evelyn Wigley**; **Prana Suhr**, Guatemala; **JeanMarie Polvino**, New York; **Omarian Atman**, California; **Mark Pountney**, Burntwood Staffs, UK; **Marisa Morin**, Ashland Oregon; **Tamera Hays**, California; Dwaine Hartman, Edmonton, Alberta; Vima Lamura, New Zealand; **Petra McGuire**, Bath, UK; **Keter Woods**, Texas; **Jason Welch**, Kauai, Hawaii, **Craig Masters**, Perth, Australia; **Daniela Knapic**, Pula, Croatia; **Maria Luisa Pinto-Pereira**, Porto, Portuagal; **Paloma Vita**, Brignogan-Plages, France; **Maria Larson**, Kalmar, Sweden; **Pilar Fernandez**, Denia-Alicante, Spain; **Carlos Molina Urizar,** Guatemala; **Diego Dougherty,** Guatemala; **Niraj Naik**, UK; **Frank Drossman**, Marienheide, Germany; **Martin Rosenberger**, Muelhiem, Germany; **Christen Rosamilia**, Grand Terrace, California; **Helen Davies,** Bayreuth, Germany; **Axel Shwekendiek** Cedar Falls, Iowa; **David Alejandro**, Mexico City, Mexico; **Joaquin Guillermo**, Palm Coast, Florida; **Natalia Morosova**, North Carolina; **Sonia Gartner**, Germany; **Val G. White**, Madison, Tennesee; **Monika Zawadzka,** Poznand Poland; **Kurt Corthout**, Leuven, Belgium; **Dixie Bowden**, Brantford, Ontario; **Sue Best**, Los Angeles, California; **JeanneChristie Drinkel**, Merseyside, UK; **John DiStefano**, Killingworth, Connecticut; **Gary Moore**, Merope USA; **Loren A. Lee;** Los Angeles, California; **Erika Yanin Perez-Hermandez,** San Jose, California; **Robin Beck, Nadine May,** South Africa; **Ana Vidal** Sao Paulo Brazil, **Antoinette O'Connell**, UK; **Dragon Light Essences**, Sao Paulo Brazil; the sound artists **amAya; Nadalokah; Source Vibrations;** and all those who have been translating the materials and supporting this project throughout, including the following members of the GoldRing site (avatar names): **Zeyani Chrisanna**, USA; **little eyes, Christina Maria; energetic heart; shantilove**, Taiwan; **artruth, filipept; Daniela.y.bg**, Bulgaria; **Pure_Windsong,** Netherlands and **coxinel007.**

www.ingramcontent.com/pod-product-compliance
Lightning Source LLC
Chambersburg PA
CBHW041121300426
44112CB00003B/47